HOW TO
BUILD GOOD
BEHAVIOR AND
SELF·ESTEEM IN
CHILDREN

HENRY D. SCHLINGER, JR.
Ph.D., BCBA-D

2021
HJH Publishing
Glendale, CA 92102

Cover design by Jay Toffoli
Cover photograph by Karl Larsen

ISBN: 9798523533280

This book is dedicated to the memory of my mentor, Dr. Jack Michael, who taught me how to analyze, and think critically about, behavior.

And to my son, Haydn, who always showed me what I did right and what I did wrong, and whom I love unconditionally.

Acknowledgements

I am eternally grateful to my wife, Julie Riggott, for her expert editing and proofreading of this book and, indeed, everything I've written. Her willingness to read the book more than once, despite her own job as an editor and writer, not to mention mother, goes above and beyond what I could expect.

Portions of this book were written with the support of a Creative Leave Award in 2015 and a Sabbatical Leave in 2016 from California State University, Los Angeles.

Table of Contents

Table of Contents

Introduction

Parents Are Behavioral Engineers

As a parent, your job is to build appropriate, productive behaviors in your children. In that sense you are kind of like an engineer — with one key difference.

Engineers use scientific principles to design and build machines and structures, like vehicles, bridges, and buildings. They use their knowledge of a group of sciences, including physics, material science, and electronics, to create blueprints and make their plans a reality.

In contrast, most parents have no plan at all, let alone one based on science.

Parents often operate on automatic pilot based on how they were raised by their own parents. They rarely understand how their behavior affects their children's behavior or how their children's behavior affects theirs. Many parents find it difficult to build good behaviors they want in their children, and they accidentally build some bad behaviors. And sometimes those bad behaviors escalate beyond the parents' control.

When they hit a roadblock, parents turn to "professionals" or "experts" or even other parents for advice. However, the advice offered by these individuals is rarely, if ever, based on behavioral science and often doesn't work.

This book teaches you how to use scientific principles to build good behavior in your children. It is really like an instruction manual for parenting in which I describe the steps by which you can increase good behavior and self-esteem and decrease undesirable behaviors in your children. In short, after going through this book, you will turn off auto pilot and take control of your own actions and feelings and those of your children.

By building good behavior in your children, you will make them happier; and if your children are happy, you will be too.

Why I Wrote This Book

When my wife suggested that I write a book about helping parents build good behavior in their children, I sat down and immediately began writing. I finished rough drafts of a couple of chapters in a few days. To me that means I was ready to write this book for some time. In my career as a behavioral psychologist, I have been a basic researcher and have applied techniques learned from such research with typically developing children, including my own child, and children with autism. I have also taught at the university level for more than 30 years and have authored numerous articles and a book on behavioral development in children.

For several years as a Professor of Psychology at Western New England University in Springfield, Massachusetts, I taught, among many other courses, a class called Child Management: Theory and Practice. In that course, as well as in the laboratory component of developmental psychology courses I taught at California State University, many students carried out projects in which they used behavioral techniques to increase desirable and decrease undesirable behaviors in children.

My experiences teaching college-level child development and parenting courses, many of which included behavior-change projects with real parents and kids, led directly to the writing of this book. Many of the examples I use in this book are actual behavior-change projects carried out by students who were parents and teachers in my university courses or by me as a consultant to families.

The Plan of the Book

The information contained in this book is based on research found in numerous scientific journals over many decades. The plan of this book is also based on decades of basic experimental research on learning.

We all know that if we simply read something, no matter how well written and interesting, it doesn't mean that our behavior will change. So, to increase the chances that you will *do* something (more than just read this book), I have designed each chapter to include several different types of learning tasks, including filling in blanks and answering other questions as you read, numerous real-life examples, and quizzes at the end of each chapter to make sure you really learn the terms and concepts. Also, I'll teach you to carry out behavior-change projects (with data collection sheets and graphs found on the book's webpage), so you can see concrete results by practicing what the book preaches: how to use scientifically based principles to build good behavior and self-esteem in children.

I've tried to organize and write the book to enhance your success. I also realize that some of the suggestions may seem counterintuitive, and you may find it difficult to carry them out. Don't be discouraged; it will work if you stick to it. If you have any questions while you are tackling a project, feel free to e-mail me from my website. I want you to succeed and I know that you can if you learn to use the principles described in this book.

Dr. Hank Schlinger
www.BuildGoodBehavior.com

Part I – The Problems and Explaining Behavior

Chapter 1: The Problems

Based on the title, the first goal of this book is to teach you to build good behavior in your children. The more you build good behavior, the less bad behavior will occur. And when your children do engage in unacceptable behavior—and they most certainly will—this book will teach you some science-based strategies for dealing with it. As a result, both you and your child will not only behave better with each other, but you will both feel better about yourselves, which achieves the second goal of the book: to build self-esteem.

My professional experience as a basic researcher, university professor, writer, parent consultant, and parent has made me a keen observer of human behavior, especially the behavior of parents and their children. And I am frequently concerned by several troublesome patterns that I see.

Five Problems

1) Parents fly on automatic pilot and are not aware of how their behavior affects their children's behavior and how their children's behavior affects theirs.

2) Parents think that just telling their kids how to behave will work.

3) Parents teach their children to be the boss.

4) Parents ignore good behavior and teach bad behavior.

5) Parents think that the kid they get is just the luck of the draw: sometimes you get a good kid and sometimes not such a good kid.

1. Flying on Automatic Pilot

The first problem is that most parents fly on automatic pilot. They are rarely aware of how they affect their kids' behavior — and misbehavior. Sometimes they may be forced to think about it, but that's usually when they feel like they're at their wits' end. Flying on automatic pilot does not usually make for happy families. The parents' failure to understand how their behavior affects their children's behavior is a major factor contributing to many problems between parents and children. This failure occurs not because parents are bad or uncaring, but because they honestly don't know any better.

Parents often find it challenging to get their children to do what they want them to do. As a result, instead of learning appropriate ways to get what they want, children often learn to act in undesirable ways. For example, many children learn to whine, pout, cry, scream, throw temper tantrums, fight, throw things, hurt themselves, or destroy property. That's right, they *learn* those things. Later, as children begin to use language, they learn how to argue, negotiate, debate, and say mean things to their parents or to their siblings or to others to get what they want, and sometimes because such behavior gets attention.

Unfortunately, in such cases, both parents and children feel bad about each other and about themselves. Children feel like they can't do anything right, and parents feel helpless and unable to make their children happy. Ironically, many of the parents' efforts to make their children happy are the very ones that contribute to their undesirable behavior and unhappiness. These parents are unknowingly caught in a trap of their own making.

For example, I knew a mother whose 3-year-old son would scream and hit her every time he didn't get his way. Even though he was only 3, his blows were hard enough to hurt. When this happened, she would try to protect herself while explaining why hitting wasn't acceptable behavior. Occasionally, she would get so angry and frustrated that she would hit him back, though not very hard. Either way, she continued to engage with him. No matter what she did, however, her son continued to hit her. She knew this was a problem and was afraid of how much worse his behavior would become as he grew older. Because these interactions took place so often, the mother was unhappy and frustrated and so was her little boy.

It turns out that the mother was unknowingly rewarding her son's hitting by talking and paying attention to him when he hit her. This mother solved her problem by using the evidenced-based methods you will learn in this book (see *Time-Out [From Positive Reinforcement]* in Chapter 7).

2. *Just Tell Him How You Want Him to Behave*

A second problem is that many parents think that the solution is just telling their children how they should act. But imagine if just telling people how to behave really worked. Just tell a person how to play the piano or how to play tennis or how to perform surgery, or even simpler things such as that they should recycle or eat healthier or exercise. Do you find yourself continuing to tell your kids to say "please" and "thank you," or to put their clothes away at night, or to do their homework, or to stop complaining or screaming or myriad other things you want them to do? As Dr. Phil famously asked, "How's that working for you?" And what about kids who are too young to understand what their parents are saying to them?

Once kids are older and can understand, it is fine to tell them what you expect of them. But even then, you have to follow up on your words: You have to show them what you want them to do and, most importantly, reward the behavior when it occurs. If you do this correctly and consistently, you can build good behavior in your children and, equally important, prevent bad behavior from being learned in the first place.

3. *Who's the Boss?*

A third problem I've noticed is that many parents are not assertive with their children. These parents indulge their children and give them everything, either thinking that will make them happy, or mostly, to get them to stop some pestering behavior. This practice almost always backfires, producing unhappy kids that some people describe as spoiled. These kids may grow up to be spoiled, unhappy adults, forcing others to wonder in bewilderment how kids who had everything could be so miserable. Obviously, they didn't have everything. In cases like these, it is as if the parents are afraid that if they state rules and consistently enforce them, and don't give in to their children's demands, their children won't like them or, worse, won't love them.

For example, one day at my son's school a mother brought her 2-year-old with her to drop off her older child. The 2-year-old had her shoes on the wrong feet, and when another mother pointed this out, the mother of the child said, "I know. I told her, but she insisted they were right." A 2-year-old insisted? Who's the boss? This example may not be a big deal—it doesn't matter whether a 2-year-old wears her shoes on the wrong feet once or twice—but it is indicative of how many parents interact with their children. Even if this example is not particularly troublesome, can you see how the interactions between this mother and child might evolve in the future as the child gets older?

Consider another example. I witnessed a mother and very young child at a concession stand. The mother said to the child, "How about we get some pita chips? Pita chips are really good!" The child loudly whined, "I want gummy worms!" The mother tried again to convince her young daughter that they should get pita chips, but the little girl continued to loudly whine that she wanted the candy. The mother finally relented saying, "Okay, you win this time." Of course, we know that the little girl always wins, at least when they are in public. Who's the boss, indeed. This mother had already given her little girl the keys to the boardroom and made her CEO by giving in and reinforcing the demands and the whining (see Appendix I, *How Oppositional and Defiant Behaviors Are Learned*).

Finally, a parent I knew was frustrated that every night her 6-year-old woke up and crawled into bed with her and her husband. She wondered if he would grow out of it, as if such behavior occurs in all kids according to some kind of timetable. Unfortunately, it's what the parents do—allowing their kid to get into bed with them—that is the problem. And no, he won't grow out of it.

Parents who are not assertive with their children and who indulge or give in to such behaviors exhibit inconsistent control, teach their children undesirable ways to get what they want, and, not surprisingly, end up with children who not only do not behave well, but are often unhappy. Children, like the rest of us, want structure. The more structured our environment is, the more structured our behavior will be and the more content we will be.

4. Ignoring Good Behavior and Teaching Bad Behavior
Perhaps the most important problem is that many parents ignore children when they are doing what the parents want them to do and instead pay attention to and, thus, reward children for inappropriate behaviors, often using ineffective measures designed to be punitive. This is the opposite of what they should do, but it is understandable. When children are behaving well, there is nothing pressing that demands the parent's attention. When children misbehave, however, such behavior immediately demands that the parents attend to the annoying behavior, if only to stop it. This book will teach you how to reverse this situation so that you will notice and reward good behavior and not reward bad behavior.

5. The Luck of the Draw
Finally, as if to simply throw up their hands and admit defeat, many parents believe that when you have a baby, you get what you get. Sometimes you get a good kid and sometimes not such a good kid. People have told me and my wife that we are lucky that our son is so good, as if having a well-behaved, or not-so-well-behaved, kid is the luck of the genetic draw. If this assumption were true—and it is not—then there would be nothing parents could do to drastically change their child's behavior. Fortunately, however, there are things you can do that work.

It's Not All Bad News
I do see some parents and teachers who intuitively do a great job, whether they know it or not, building and encouraging good behavior in children. As a result, both the parents and the kids are happy. For example, one day in a store I saw a mother pushing a

cart with her newborn, and even though the infant was only a month or two old, the mother was talking to her. Now, obviously, the infant didn't understand what the mother was saying, nor could she participate in a "conversation." However, by talking to her infant the mother was accomplishing two things. First, she was engaging with her infant and rewarding her for looking at the mother. And second, she was doing what all parents should do all the time with their infants: talk to them in approving ways (see Chapter 14, *Talking and Reading to Your Infant*).

In another example of good parenting, I witnessed a mother at a table in a restaurant with her three preadolescent children. She spent the entire time talking to all of them. Because these children were older, there was a lively conversation lasting the entire meal. Contrast this with many parents who give their children tablets or smart phones when they go out and hardly, if ever, interact with them. Whether she knew it or not, the mother in this example was rewarding acceptable and appropriate behavior and preventing any unacceptable behavior from occurring. Of course, as with the mother and the newborn in the preceding example, this mother was also providing a good model of language—and parenting.

Unfortunately, these examples of good parenting are not as frequent as they should be. Moreover, relationships built on the correct use of the scientifically based behavioral principles that you will learn in this book are not as common as they could or should be.

Solutions

When parents are at their wits' end, they seek solutions. When what they've been doing isn't working, parents often turn to others for help, whether it is parenting books or magazines, advice columns, friends, so-called parenting "experts," "life coaches," or medical doctors (e.g., pediatricians). Unfortunately, many of the recommended solutions don't work, and they often cost money, sometimes a lot!

Buy a Book, Take a Class, or Consult an "Expert"

As you know, there are dozens of books in the Psychology, Self-Help, or Parenting sections of bookstores (and on the Internet). Many of these books promise to teach parents how to handle specific problem behaviors, such as sleep problems. But because those problems are so different from child to child or from family to family, it is very difficult to provide a cookbook approach that will work for everyone. If one prescribed solution doesn't work, what do you do, buy a book for every single problem you want to solve? Also, many parenting books, even those by physicians or clinicians, are not based on a science of behavior, but rather on unsupported theories or personal experience and anecdotes. While some of their suggestions might work for a few people, there's no guarantee.

A much more effective alternative is to provide parents with some general problem-solving skills based on a science of behavior so they can apply them to any problem behavior. Such an approach can give you more control and allow you to experiment until the problem is solved. That is the approach taken in this book.

Many cities, churches, and even schools offer classes for parents. It's hard to evaluate them because there are so many, but what I will say is that if the advice being peddled in these classes is not based on science, then the advice is probably not very reliable. If those teaching classes are therapists or other parents, then the advice offered is usually just anecdotal or based on what the teacher thinks is common sense. Either way, as a parent, you might feel good in the class, like you might feel at a motivational seminar, but when you leave and go back home, you face the same behavioral problems you did before the class.

There are also numerous so-called "experts" on the radio and television and in newspapers and on the Internet — many with all kinds of letters after their names, and some who are just parents relaying anecdotal experiences — all offering advice to parents on how to improve their children's behavior. Worse, there are many types of modern-day snake oils, from wearing colored lenses to "cure" autism or dyslexia to taking herbal supplements that are offered — for a price — to change behaviors. Of course, drugs such as Ritalin and Adderall are prescribed to millions of children. These "cures" seem to involve easy fixes and, therefore, are tempting. We live in a culture that puts a premium on quick fixes, and that is what many of us have come to expect.

When it comes to building good behavior in children, however, there are several adages that apply. For example, "If it's worth doing, it's worth doing right," and "No pain, no gain." There are no silver bullets; nothing comes easy, and you have to work hard to improve behavior. Moreover, advice based on good experimental research is always going to be more successful than advice based on logic alone, badly conducted research, testimonials, or personal or professional anecdotes, even if they are based on the experience of a clinician, therapist, or pediatrician.

Who You Gonna Call?

Pediatricians are a frequent go-to for parents who have concerns about their children's behavior, but pediatricians are not behavioral scientists or even behavioral specialists. They are medical doctors, and most are not trained to know where to refer parents of children with behavioral problems. Some pediatricians (think of Drs. Spock, Brazelton, or Sears) have become household names not because of their medical expertise, but because of their behavioral advice.

People who have direct experience with kids, such as physicians, clinicians, therapists, teachers, and even parents, gain a certain kind of knowledge about those kids and their behavior. But it is not the same as scientific knowledge. We all know how to drive our cars and even basically how the car works, but very few of us know enough to diagnose and fix a car when it has problems. We turn to professional mechanics. Parents know a lot about their kids' health, but when it comes to diagnosing and treating a medical problem, they seek professional medical advice. The same should be true with behavior. Parents should turn to behavior scientists not only to fix behavior when it is broken, but more importantly, to prevent it from breaking in the first place. This instruction manual will teach you step-by-step how to build good behaviors in your children and, as a result, self-esteem. Look at it as a way to improve the behavioral health of your children.

You Need to Discipline Her!

Many people will tell you that the solution for children who misbehave is that they just need more discipline. I couldn't agree more. However, for most people the word *discipline* means punishment, as in "You'd better discipline her for talking back." In fact, the word *discipline* comes from the word *disciple*, meaning one who teaches. For example, Jesus' disciples promoted his teachings to others. Likewise, parents who use discipline correctly are teaching their children. Parents are their children's first and most influential and important teachers. As many psychologists know, one doesn't teach by using threats or punishment, but by using positive reinforcement. This book will teach you how to discipline your children based on the literal meaning of the word: to teach.

Before moving on, try this brief quiz. You will find many of the answers to quiz questions in bold or italics in the chapters.

Quiz 1

1. The first goal of this book is to teach you how to _____ good behavior.

2. The second goal of this book is to build _____-_____ in your children.

3. One common parenting problem is that parents fly on _____ _____, which means that parents are not usually aware of how their behavior affects their kids' behavior.

4. Perhaps the most important problem is that parents _____ good behavior and instead _____ bad behavior.

5. Another common problem is that parents are not _____ with their children and end up indulging and giving in to all kinds of behaviors—good and bad.

6. In the two examples of good parenting, both mothers rewarded good behavior in their infant and adolescents respectively simply by _____ with them.

7. True or False? Just telling your kids how you want them to behave will work to get them to behave. _____

8. When parents are at their wits' end, and have tried everything they know, they end up calling their child's _____.

9. The problem with most medical doctors is that while they are medical experts, they are not _____ experts.

10. The word *discipline* literally means to _____.

Quiz 1 Answers

1. The first goal of this book is to teach you how to *build* good behavior.

2. The second goal of this book is to build *self-esteem* in your children.

3. One common parenting problem is that parents fly on *automatic pilot*, which means that parents are not usually aware of how their behavior affects their kids' behavior.

4. Perhaps the most important problem is that parents *ignore* good behavior and instead *reward* bad behavior.

5. Another common problem is that parents are not *assertive* with their children and end up indulging and giving in to all kinds of behaviors—good and bad.

6. In the two examples of good parenting, both mothers rewarded good behavior in their infant and adolescents respectively simply by *talking* with them.

7. True or False? Just telling your kids how you want them to behave will work to get them to behave. *False*

8. When parents are at their wits' end, and have tried everything they know, they end up calling their child's *pediatrician*.

9. The problem with most medical doctors is that while they are medical experts, they are not *behavioral* experts.

10. The word *discipline* literally means to *teach*.

Chapter 2: Causes and Explanations of Behavior

Before getting into the details of how to build good behavior, I need to address faulty explanations of behavior because if we explain behavior incorrectly, it is much harder to change it. We often explain why people behave the way they do by appealing to causes that are vague and nonexistent. For example, it is frequently said that a child hits another child *because he is aggressive*; or a child speaks softly *because she is shy*; or a child throws a tantrum *because she is strong willed or is in the terrible-two stage*; or a child doesn't do what his parents tell him to do *because he is oppositional*; or a child interrupts her parents' conversation *because she is rude*; or a child cries when the parent leaves the room *because he has separation anxiety*.

All these explanations — aggression, shyness, strong will, terrible twos, oppositional, rudeness, separation anxiety — and many more, point to vague things that children supposedly have inside them that cause them to behave the way they do.

These explanations also reflect an ingrained belief about why people, especially children, do what they do, namely that they choose to behave in certain ways and are therefore responsible for their behavior. This belief that behavior somehow comes from within the individual constitutes a kind of philosophy about human behavior that we all share. Our parents and others implicitly taught this philosophy to us, and we pass it on to our children. Moreover, this philosophy is codified by such academic disciplines as psychology and other soft sciences as well as our educational system. In my view, it is this philosophy that in large part prevents us from effectively dealing with problem behavior and from effectively teaching our children.

In addition to the examples mentioned above, there are similar explanations that seem to be exceptions in that they presumably point to things that are more real and much more serious, such as attention deficit hyperactivity disorder (ADHD), autism, oppositional defiant disorder (ODD), dyslexia, and so on. You will recognize these explanations as names of disorders that people believe some children have and that cause them to behave in certain ways. Even though we are told that these explanations represent real disorders, I will argue that much of the time they are no better than the other explanations mentioned above that appeal to vague things inside the child.

In this chapter, I want to teach you a more scientific way of thinking about behavior and give you some practice looking at behavior in this manner. It is not mandatory that you change your philosophy about your child's behavior to benefit from the practical problem-solving strategies described in this book, but it will certainly help.

Faulty Explanations of Behavior

Most of the ways we typically explain behavior are faulty because they do not point to real causes. As a result, they are not helpful if we want to change behavior. Consider an example. Janie cries and screams whenever her parents ask her to do something. When asked why she cries and screams, we are told it's *because she is oppositional*, or has ODD.

Such an explanation sounds reasonable, until we ask one very important question: "What evidence do we have, or how do we know, that Janie is oppositional?" Of course, the only evidence is that she cries and screams when asked to do something. But those are the very behaviors we want to explain in the first place. So, basically, we have given a name to her behaviors of crying and screaming— *oppositional* —and then used that name to explain them. You shouldn't be surprised to learn that this is a type of faulty explanation called *circular reasoning* or *circular explanation*.

A circular explanation is one in which the evidence for the explanation is the same as the behavior you want to explain. Once you learn to recognize circular explanations, you'll find that they are everywhere.

Let's look at another example. Suppose Mario has trouble paying attention in class. He is easily distractible, behaves impulsively, and often gets up out of his seat. When asked why he does these things, his teacher, parents, and pediatrician explain that it is *because he has ADHD*. Before we accept this explanation, we should stop and ask an important question: "What evidence do we have, or how do we know, that Mario has ADHD?" I hope you already know where we're going with this. Of course, the answer is the very same behaviors we want to explain — he is inattentive, easily distractible, impulsive, and overly active.

So, ADHD is an example of a _____ explanation that doesn't explain the behaviors at all. In this example, like the previous example of Janie being oppositional, we have simply given a name to a certain set of behaviors—ADHD— and then used that name to explain the very same behaviors. In the case of ADHD, the name is actually a list of the behaviors— attention deficit and hyperactivity. In the end, we still don't know why Mario is inattentive, easily distractible, impulsive, and very active.

The biggest problem with circular and other faulty explanations is that they don't point to the real causes of behavior. As such, when we want to change the behavior, we have nothing to work with. For example, how do we change Janie's oppositional behavior or Mario's ADHD (except by using medication)? In fact, if we can get Janie not to cry and scream and can get Mario to sit still and pay attention — which we most definitely can — without medication, then we wouldn't say they are oppositional or have ADHD anymore. Do you see the circularity in these explanations?

To help you identify circular explanations, here are four questions you can ask.

1. "What behavior do you want to explain (or change)?"

In the case of Janie, it is crying and screaming. For Mario, it is his inattentiveness, getting up out of his seat, and behaving impulsively. Answering this question requires that we identify the actual behaviors that we observe and want to explain (which I will teach you how to do in Chapter 8).

2. "What is the explanation offered for the observed behavior?"

The answer to this question is the answer to *why* the child engages in the behavior and usually follows the word *because* (which is derived from *by cause of*) in a sentence. For example, Janie cries and screams *because* she is oppositional. So, the explanation we were given for Janie's behavior is that she is oppositional. The explanation we were given for Mario's behavior is that he has ADHD.

3. "What is the evidence for the explanation?" In other words, how do you know that Janie is oppositional or that Mario has ADHD?

The evidence that Janie is oppositional is that she cries and screams when asked to do something. The evidence that Mario has ADHD is that he gets up out of his seat and is inattentive in class. There is no other evidence. We do not diagnose ODD or ADHD with brain scans or blood tests, only the presenting behavior(s).

4. "Is the evidence (for the explanation) the very same behaviors you want to explain in the first place?"

If the answer to this question is "yes," which it is in both examples, then you have a circular explanation, which, I hope you have realized by now, is not an explanation at all.

Before we go on, I should point out that in many, if not most, instances, the behaviors associated with both ADHD and ODD are learned. In Appendix I, I will describe how oppositional behaviors are learned and often lead to antisocial and aggressive behaviors. And I will offer one explanation as to why so many kids seem to have ADHD in schools.

Now try your hand at these examples to see which ones are circular.

- Carla screams "No!" whenever her parents ask her to do something. When asked why, we are told it is *because she has ODD.*
  - This explanation is circular because the only evidence for the __ __ __ is the same as Carla's behavior of _____
  _____.

- When David reads, he says "b" when he sees "d." We are told that he does this *because he has dyslexia.*
  - This explanation is circular because the only evidence for the dyslexia is simply David's behavior of saying
  _____.

- In the same example, we are told that David says "b" when he sees "d" *because he has trouble processing visual information.*
  - This explanation is circular because the only evidence for the trouble _____ visual information is the same as David's behavior of saying _____
  _____.

- Donald throws a tantrum in the store with his father. Someone says he does this *because he gets attention* from the father.
  - This explanation is NOT circular because the evidence for getting _____ from the father when Donald throws a tantrum is NOT the same as the behavior of _____.

- Jordan always complies with her parents' requests. Her parents say she does this *because she wants to please them.*
  - This explanation is circular because the only evidence that Jordan wants to _____ her parents is simply the same as her behavior of _____.

- Chuck hits another child, and a psychologist explains that he does this *because he has an aggressive personality.*
  - This explanation is circular because the only evidence for the _____ personality is the same as his behavior of _____.

- Someone else, however, says that Chuck hits another child *because he gets the toy he wants.*

o This explanation is NOT circular because the evidence for getting the _____ is NOT the same as the behavior of _____.

Now let's see how you did. In the first example, the explanation is circular because the only evidence for the ODD is Carla screaming "No!" when asked to do something. The explanations of dyslexia and trouble processing in the second and third examples are circular because the only evidence for them is the behavior of saying "b" when seeing "d." The explanation of attention for the tantrum in the fourth example is NOT circular because the evidence for the attention is not the behavior of throwing a tantrum, that is, we can observe Donald getting attention separately from the behavior of throwing a tantrum. In the fifth example, the explanation of wanting to please is circular again because the only evidence for Jordan wanting to please her parents is that she complies with their requests. In the next to last example, the explanation — aggressive personality — is circular because the only evidence for Chuck aggressive personality is his behavior of hitting. And in the last example, the explanation of getting the toy is NOT circular because we can observe Chuck getting the toy independently of his behavior of hitting.

Genes and the Brain

There are other faulty explanations of behavior that are also sometimes circular. Nowadays we often hear that behavior is caused by genes or the brain. Of course, in one sense this is true. Were it not for the genes we inherit from our parents and our central nervous system (brain and spinal cord), we would not have any behavior — or anything else for that matter. But when we are told that some gene or some part of the brain causes behavior, we are on thin ice.

First of all, most of the time there is no direct evidence of the gene or brain structure; that is, no one has ever observed them. But even if there is some direct evidence, we can't do anything about it. There is no way right now to permanently alter one's genes or brain to change behavior. Meanwhile, research has shown that the types of learning experiences I talk about in this book actually alter the brain chemistry!

So, you might ask, "What are we left with?" Even though explanations in terms of genes or the brain may point to possible causes of behavior, which, at present, they don't, there is nothing we can do about them if we want to change behavior.

Where Does Behavior Come From?

The examples of explanations of behavior provided above stem from a way that we talk about behavior that I have referred to as a kind of simple philosophy of behavior that we learned from our parents. It is an intuitive philosophy in the sense that we do not give much, if any, thought to it. We didn't learn it in any formal manner; it is simply the way most of us have learned to talk about behavior.

This philosophy basically assumes that behavior comes from within the individual, from his or her mind, thoughts, wishes, desires, intentions, personality, motivations, ideas, genes or brain, etc. In other words, we believe that each of us chooses to behave, whether consciously or not; and, as a result, we are ultimately responsible and should be given credit or blame for our own behavior. This might make sense for older children and adults who can reason about their own behavior, but it makes little sense for infants or younger children. (Just so you know, I don't believe that this philosophy makes sense for anyone.) But if behavior doesn't come from within the individual, then where does it come from?

It's the Environment, Stupid

Leading up to the 1992 presidential election, George H. W. Bush was ahead in the polls when challenger Bill Clinton began to utter the phrase, "It's the economy, stupid." This one phrase focused everyone's attention on the most important problem facing the nation, and, perhaps not coincidentally, Clinton was elected. When talking about human behavior, a similar phrase is apropos: "It's the environment, stupid." Just as Bill Clinton's original phrase focused attention on the economy, our paraphrase focuses attention on the _____. But what do we mean by "environment"?

For most people, the environment consists of their surroundings, which include such things as the families and neighborhoods in which they are raised, or whether they have one or two parents and siblings, or the schools they attend. And while such conceptions are not entirely incorrect, they are not the same as a scientific view of the ***environment***, which states simply that it consists of ***all the moment-to-moment events that affect a person's behavior***. These events can come from the child's interactions with other people or from the physical environment.

Consider an example of the development of reaching and grasping in infants. At about 6 months of age, very young infants begin to reach out and attempt to grasp things. But these skills do not just spring out of nowhere. In the beginning, the infant's efforts are extremely clumsy and uncoordinated, as all their behavior is.

Infants learn to reach and grasp as they constantly try to manipulate things. The environment for the infant is the moment-to-moment changes that happen as the infant moves his or her hand in myriad ways. Some of those ways are more successful in touching or reaching and grasping objects, and some are less successful. But the number of different variations on the behavior are staggeringly high; and the number of changes in stimulation that result from all those different behavioral variations, including visual, tactile, and proprioceptive feedback (that is, about the movement of the body), are also staggeringly high. In other words, not only does the infant see her hand getting near and/or touching the object, she also feels the object on or in her hand, etc. It is only after a lot of experience with objects (literally thousands of interactions) that infants' clumsy behavior becomes refined and coordinated, and they are able to reach and grasp an object with ease. Of course, we are not aware of all these individual interactions. We just notice one day that our infant can reach out and grasp objects and wonder how she was able to do this.

In this example, it is common to say that the infant *figured out* how to reach and grasp, or that she now *understands* how to reach and grasp. But without the thousands of individual interactions between her behavior and her environment, she would not have figured it out or understood what to do. Saying that she figured out or now understands what to do is circular in that the only evidence of her understanding is that she now can reach and grasp. In this example, it is the visual, tactile, and proprioceptive consequences of her behavior from the environment that shaped her initially clumsy and uncoordinated behaviors into finely tuned reaching and grasping. Just like a sculptor shapes an unformed piece of clay into a vase, the environment shapes our behavior.

Our seemingly simple definition of environment has several advantages over traditional nonscientific conceptions. The most important advantage is that the events that make up the environment are observable and testable; we don't have to take someone's word for anything. For example, if we claim that a child's tantrum is caused by the attention the child receives when he tantrums, we can test that explanation. After we observe the attention, we can stop giving it to see if the tantrum changes.

Our more scientific concept of the environment also has at least two important implications for understanding behavior that differ from traditional views. The first is that the environment constantly changes. The traditional view is that the environment is static — the same house, the same parents, etc. A person's environment, however, is different moment to moment.

The second implication of our definition is that the environment cannot be the same for any two individuals. Sometimes parents ask me how their children can be so different from one another even though they were raised in the same environment. Such questions imply that these differences between their children in personality and behavior must be genetic because they had the same environment (i.e., parents, house, etc.). But the flaw in this question is the assumption that the children share the same environment. If environment consists of *all the moment-to-moment events that affect behavior*, then no two people can ever possibly have the same environment. And the environment can be wildly different for two individuals, even identical twins.

Both of these implications are important for our more scientific view of behavior because they suggest that the environment is the primary cause of both good and bad behavior. Because the environment is observable, we can change it to improve behavior.

The Kid Is Always Right

Scientific psychologists have a saying that has profound implications for how we view behavior: ***The kid is always right***. This doesn't mean that everything kids do is appropriate or desirable or that we like everything they do. It means that there is a cause of their behaviors, whether they are good or bad. So, if a child says "b" when he sees "d," this is obviously wrong from our point of view, but there is a reason (i.e., a cause) why the child does this (and it's not dyslexia—that is only a name for the behavior, and using it to explain the behavior would be circular). Or if a kid throws a tantrum, it is clearly not a desirable behavior, but there is a cause of the tantrum (and it's not because the kid is in the terrible-two stage). The cause does not come from within the kid, but from the environment.

If we look at the causes of children's behaviors in the moment-to-moment events that constitute their environment, we'll find that the responsibility for the child's behavior doesn't rest with the child. One of the main points of this book is that the child's behavior is caused by the environment. A not-so-obvious conclusion, then, is that we don't give the child credit or blame for his or her behaviors. In other words: ***Kids are not good or bad; their behavior is***.

Of course, the distinction between what is good and bad is largely a cultural one because what is viewed as desirable in one culture may be considered undesirable in another culture. This conception of a child's behavior also means that we don't try to change children. We try to change their behavior. As we will see, this means that we don't reward or punish kids. We reward or punish their behaviors.

Before moving on, try this brief quiz.

Quiz 2

1. We all learned a kind of simple philosophy about behavior: Behavior comes from within the _____.

2. When the evidence for an explanation is the same as the behavior you want to explain, this is called a _____ explanation.

3. If we say that a child is inattentive, impulsive, and overly active *because* she has ADHD, this is a _____ explanation IF the only evidence for her ADHD is that she is inattentive, impulsive, and overly active.

4. When talking about the causes of children's behaviors, it is important to remember the phrase "It's the _____, stupid," because it focuses our attention on their _____, not their genes or brain.

5. The definition of _____ is *all of the moment-to-moment events that affect a person's behavior.*

6. When we find ourselves tempted to blame a kid for his or her bad behavior, we should remember the phrase: "The kid is always _____," which doesn't mean that what the kid has done is desirable, only that there is a _____ for it.

7. "Kids are not good or bad. Their _____ is."

8. Based on our definition of environment, it is safe to say that the environment is never the _____ for any two individuals.

9. If it is true that children are not responsible for their own behavior, then they can never really deserve _____ for their good behaviors or _____ for their bad behaviors.

10. Because most of the ways we explain behavior do not point to the real causes of behavior, these explanations are _____.

Quiz 2 Answers

1. We all learned a kind of simple philosophy about behavior: Behavior comes from within the *individual (or person or child)*.

2. When the evidence for an explanation is the same as the behavior you want to explain, this is called a *circular* explanation.

3. If we say that a child is inattentive, impulsive, and overly active *because* she has ADHD, this is a *circular* explanation IF the only evidence for her ADHD is that she is inattentive, impulsive, and overly active.

4. When talking about the causes of children's behaviors, it is important to remember the phrase "It's the *environment*, stupid," because it focuses our attention on their *environment*, not their genes or brain.

5. The definition of *environment* is *all of the moment-to-moment events that affect a person's behavior*.

6. When we find ourselves tempted to blame a kid for his or her bad behavior, we should remember the phrase: "The kid is always *right*," which doesn't mean that what the kid has done is desirable, only that there is a *cause* for it.

7. "Kids are not good or bad. Their *behavior* is."

8. Based on our definition of environment, it is safe to say that the environment is never the *same* for any two individuals.

9. If it is true that children are not responsible for their own behavior, then they can never really deserve *credit* for their good behaviors or *blame* for their bad behaviors.

10. Because most of the ways we explain behavior do not point to the real causes of behavior, these explanations are *faulty*.

Part II – What Is Reinforcement, and What Makes It Work?

Chapter 3: What Is Reinforcement?

In the previous chapter, I stated that the environment is the primary cause of our behaviors. But what exactly about the environment causes behavior? In general, there are two reasons why kids (and adults) do what they do. The first reason is that their behavior gets them something they want — like attention from others, toys or other objects, activities such as playing outside or playing video games, or simply stimulation from the environment (e.g., the TV going on and off when a remote-control button is pushed). The second reason is that their behavior gets them out of doing something they do not want to do, such as homework, chores, or, for some kids, anything their parents or others ask them to do. As we will see later, this applies to the parents' behavior as well. For example, sometimes the parent behaves to escape their kids' annoying whining and crying.

Behavioral psychologists have a name for these two general causes of behavior: *reinforcement*. The term reinforcement has entered the popular lexicon, but it is often talked about incorrectly. So, what is reinforcement?

Reinforcement Defined

Reinforcement is the name given to one of the very few scientific laws discovered by psychologists. Reinforcement is called a *law* because it applies universally. That means it affects the behavior of most species — but especially the behavior of human beings — in predictable ways.

In simple terms, ***reinforcement* is an outcome of a behavior that makes that behavior MORE likely to happen again in similar circumstances**. The verb "to reinforce" means *to strengthen*, so it is appropriate to say that reinforcement _____*s* the behavior it follows in similar circumstances.

Using reinforcement is like saying, "Do it again." For example, if your child gets ready for bed when you ask her to and you say, "Thank you for getting ready for bed when I asked," it's like saying, "Please get ready again the next time I ask you." In this example, saying "thank you" is an *outcome* of your daughter's *behavior* of doing what you asked, *and* if she is more likely to comply with a request from you *in similar circumstances* (when she is again asked to go to bed), then we call saying "thank you" a _____*er* for her behavior. (If you said "reinforcer" you are correct.)

Now, you might ask, "Why should I have to thank my daughter for doing something I asked her to do and that she should do anyway?" The answer is that if she does not already do that when you ask her, then you'll want to use the methods described in this book. These methods will work, and they will result in both you and your daughter feeling better about each other.

Two Kinds of Reinforcement

Behavioral scientists have discovered two kinds of reinforcement: positive and negative. Positive doesn't mean good, and negative doesn't mean bad. They are both good in the sense that we want them. **Positive means that something is added** (or given or presented), as in addition (+). **Negative means that something is subtracted** (or withdrawn, or removed, or taken away), as in subtraction (-). So, positive reinforcement is an event that is *added* after a behavior and makes the behavior *more* likely to occur again *under similar circumstances*. And negative reinforcement is an event that is *subtracted* (or removed) after a behavior and makes the behavior *more* likely to occur again *under similar circumstances*. Although I will talk about both types in this book, I will focus mostly on positive reinforcement.

Positive Reinforcement

Remember that with positive reinforcement, some event is _____ after a behavior and the behavior is _____ likely to happen again the next time the circumstances are similar.

Reinforcement occurs for every behavior we engage in. Often, the reinforcers themselves are not easy to identify because they are not what most people think of as reinforcement. Most people think reinforcement involves the intentional use of praise, candy, gold stars, etc., that are given to someone for a job well done.

Most people use the terms *reward* and *reinforcement* synonymously. But, unlike the term *reinforcement, reward* doesn't focus on whether behavior is more likely to occur again in similar circumstances, which is the defining feature of reinforcement. Many things that people use as rewards (e.g., money, praise, gold stars, points, etc.) do not necessarily make the behavior more likely to occur again in similar circumstances. If they don't make behavior more likely to occur, then they are not reinforcers.

Many events that are reinforcers defy the common-sense view of reward. Following are some examples. For each example, try to imagine what would happen if the reinforcing consequence (i.e., the reinforcer) didn't occur (i.e., it wasn't added).

• As I type on the computer to write this book, letters appear on the screen. Seeing the letters makes it _____ likely that I'll press the letter keys the next time I want to type.

• When your daughter presses the on switch for her video game, the game immediately comes on. That makes it _____ likely that she'll press the on switch the next time she wants to play the game.

• When I walk down the street and say "hi" to someone and that person smiles and says "hi" back, I *may* be _____ likely to say "hi" to other people when walking down the street.

• When your daughter grabs a toy away from her little brother and immediately gets the toy, she *may* be _____ likely to yank toys away from him when she wants them.

• When your infant drops a toy on the floor and you immediately pick it up and give it back to him, he *may* be _____ likely to drop it again.

In each of these examples, *if* adding a consequence following some behavior (seeing letters appear on the screen after typing, having a video gave come on after pressing the on switch, having people say "hi" when I say "hi," getting a toy after yanking it away) makes that behavior *more* likely to occur when circumstances are similar, then the behavior has been *positively reinforced.* But in each of these cases, no one has intentionally praised or acknowledged the behavior or given anything special to the person.

In these, and most, examples, the reinforcement is what we call **automatic** in that it is either not given by another person or not given consciously or intentionally. An important point to understand is that a reinforcer is not defined by what it looks like or how it feels, but rather how it works, namely, to make some behavior _____ likely to occur again under _____ circumstances.

Also, notice that in some of the examples listed above, I said that the consequence *may* make the behavior more likely to occur again under similar circumstances. This is because there are always other factors that work alongside reinforcement that influence whether, or how much, it works. These other factors will be discussed in Chapter 4. And, of course, it's always possible that in the above examples the behavior may not be more likely to occur again under similar circumstances. If it isn't, then the consequence/outcome cannot be called a reinforcer.

Negative Reinforcement
This book focuses primarily on how to effectively use positive reinforcement to build good behavior. But negative reinforcement is as ubiquitous as positive reinforcement, and because so many of us (inadvertently) use negative reinforcement to get our kids (and others) to behave, it is important that you understand it fully. Remember that in negative reinforcement a consequence is subtracted (or removed or withdrawn) after a behavior, which makes the behavior more likely to occur under similar circumstances. Consider the following examples of how negative reinforcement occurs in our natural environments.
- The window is open, and someone starts using a chainsaw next door. You immediately close the window. The behavior of closing the window is _____*ly reinforced* by <u>removing or subtracting</u> the loud noise of the chainsaw. And *you are more likely to close the window* the next time you hear a loud chain saw (or other loud noise).

- You hurt a muscle working out, and you put ice on it, which immediately reduces the pain. The behavior of putting ice on the sore muscle is _____*ly reinforced* because the pain is immediately <u>subtracted or removed</u>. The behavior of putting ice on a sore muscle is _____ likely to occur again.
- Once the temperature in your house reaches 80 degrees F, you turn on the air conditioner. The behavior of turning on the air conditioner is *negatively*_____ by <u>removing</u> the heat and is _____ likely to happen again when the temperature is hot.
- The telephone rings and rings while you are eating dinner, so you finally answer it. The behavior of answering the telephone is _____*ly* _____*ed* by having the ringing immediately <u>stop (i.e., it is subtracted)</u>. Therefore, the behavior of _____ the telephone is more likely to happen the next time the _____ _____ when you are having dinner.
- Your car alarm sounds, and you immediately push the remote button to turn it off. Having the alarm immediately <u>stop</u> sounding _____*ly* _____*es* the behavior of pushing the remote button. So, the next time your car alarm sounds, you are more likely to _____ .

- Your infant cries and you immediately give him a bottle. He stops crying. Having the crying stop _____*ly* _____*es* your behavior of giving the bottle the next time he cries.

The first thing to notice about these examples of negative reinforcement from the natural world is that no one intentionally removed anything after another person's behavior. In other words, they are *automatic negative reinforcers*.

A second thing to notice about any example of negative reinforcement is that some situation was first made unpleasant (the sound of a chain saw, muscle pain, heat, ringing telephone, car alarm, infant crying) before you could behave in some way to remove the unpleasantness. You don't like these things, and you will usually do whatever it takes to terminate them. But you *do* like turning them off, so contrary to common belief, *negative reinforcement is a good thing, and people like it.*

A third thing to notice is that the actual (negative) reinforcer is the *removal* or *subtraction* of the unpleasant event, not the event itself. So, it is the removal of the sound of the chainsaw, telephone, car alarm, infant crying, muscle pain, and heat that reinforces or strengthens the behaviors that removed them, making those behaviors more likely to occur again under similar circumstances.

Negative reinforcement is also a natural part of our world, but because of its unpleasant side effects (see below), I do not recommend that you use it with your children. Having said that, it is almost impossible to never use negative reinforcement. But if you are aware of what it is, you might be able to minimize it in your interactions with your children.

Now that you have seen examples of both positive and negative reinforcement, let's consider a slightly more complex example, which includes them both. The following occurs countless times every day in stores all over the country.

- A parent and child go into a store. The child <u>cries and screams</u> for candy. The parent, embarrassed and frustrated, <u>gives</u> the child candy, and the child stops crying. Both are much happier as a result. Or are they?

In this example, both the child's and parent's behaviors are being reinforced. Here's how. The child's crying and screaming are reinforced (strengthened) by the *addition* of the candy — a positive reinforcer — because the next time the parent and child are in the store (similar circumstances), the child will be more likely to _____. (If you said, "cry and scream," you're right.)

But reinforcement is not a one-way street. The parent's behavior of giving the candy is also reinforced (strengthened) by the *subtraction* of the crying — a negative reinforcer — because the next time the parent and child are in the store <u>and</u> the child cries and screams for candy (similar circumstances), the parent will be more likely to _____. (If you said, "give the child candy," you're right again.)

A helpful way to think about this example is to ask what the child wants and what the parent wants. The child wants candy, and the parent wants the crying and screaming to stop. So, they both do what it takes to get what they want. Unfortunately, both the child and the parent reinforce each other's behavior, meaning they are more likely to do the same things again under similar circumstances. And they both feel bad as a result.

It is important to note that in most instances, neither the parent nor the child is aware that they're reinforcing each other's behavior, but they are, and in ways that are not desirable for either of them. The child doesn't feel good having to cry and scream to get candy. And the parent certainly doesn't feel good hearing the child cry and scream, especially in public, or giving in to the crying and screaming. If the parent was aware of how reinforcement works, he or she could avoid this kind of unpleasant interaction in the future. This book will try to teach you to be more aware of these types of situations, how to change them, and, more importantly, how to prevent them.

Reinforcement Is a Two-Way Street

The preceding example illustrates a very important point: **Parents and children reinforce each other's behaviors all the time.** In other words, the relationship is reciprocal. In fact, every time any two (or more) people interact, they are reinforcing (and sometimes punishing — see Chapter 7) each other's behaviors. That is what maintains the interaction (or not). I point this out so that parents will understand that it is always a two-way street. However, because the parents are the adults, it is their responsibility to foster any changes in the dynamics of the interactions.

It is also important to understand that both positive and negative reinforcement can be used to strengthen the same behavior. Consider the following example:

- Father A asks his daughter, "Please pick up your toys," and immediately after she does so, the father says, "Thank you

for doing what I asked. You can now go outside and play."
If his daughter is more likely to pick up her toys when her
father asks in the future, then her behavior has been
positively _____ *ed* (i.e., strengthened) by the
father's "thank you."

Notice that in this example, positive reinforcement (praise
and activity) was *added* after the daughter picked up her toys. In
this example, the daughter gets something she wants — the
father's attention and to go outside and play — and the father gets
what he wants — his daughter's compliance. When this happens,
both the child and father feel good about themselves. Moreover,
they both feel good about each other. However, this is not
necessarily so with negative reinforcement, as the following
example shows.

- Father B nags his daughter to clean up her room, and when
  she finally does, he stops nagging. If his daughter is more
  likely to clean her room in the future when her father nags,
  then cleaning her room has been *negatively*
  _____ *ed* by the subtraction of the nagging
  right after she starts to clean her room.

In this example, the father (probably unknowingly) stops
his nagging when his daughter starts to clean her room because she
has done what he asked her to do. However, in order to use
negative reinforcement (removing the nagging), the father had to
make things unpleasant for his daughter in the first place, by
nagging. Notice that in this example, father and daughter still get
what they want. The daughter gets her father to stop nagging (by
cleaning her room when he nags), and the father gets his
daughter's compliance by nagging her until she complies. Notice,
however, that the daughter could have also gotten what she wanted
— getting rid of the father's nagging — by closing her bedroom
door and cranking up the stereo, or by leaving the house. But in
this instance, neither the father nor the child is happy. The child
will complain that "My Dad always nags me," and the father is
likely to complain that "I have to nag Sarah to get her to do what I
want."

As this last point shows, even though negative reinforcement, by definition, can be as effective as positive reinforcement, it might strengthen behaviors other than the desired one, that is, any behaviors that will subtract or remove the unpleasant event (see Appendix I for a discussion of how some parents inadvertently use negative reinforcement to shape oppositional and aggressive behavior).

Also, if you use negative reinforcement often, it might make your children resent and feel bad about you and may make them want to escape or avoid you (another way for them to subtract the unpleasant event). In the example above, turning up the stereo or leaving the house escapes the father's nagging and both are _____ likely to recur the next time he nags her. Moreover, the daughter might try to avoid her father in the future. And even if she is unsuccessful, she won't feel very good about him, or him about her, because he has to nag just to get her to comply with a simple request.

Unfortunately, this is how many of us interact with others every day. One more point about these examples: Notice that the father and daughter's behaviors are dependent on one another and neither occurs in a vacuum. This is true all the time. Even when we are alone, our behavior is dependent on the natural environment as the previous examples of both positive and negative reinforcement showed. Remember: "It's the environment, stupid!"

You Can't Judge a Book by Its Cover

Before continuing, I must clarify something. You can't tell what a reinforcer is just by looking at it. **In order to tell whether some outcome of a behavior is in fact a *reinforcer*, you must be able to show that it has indeed strengthened (or increased) the behavior it immediately follows <u>in similar circumstances</u>.**

So, what do we mean by "similar circumstances"? The question you need to ask is, "The next time there is an opportunity for the behavior to occur AND the individual wants the reinforcer (the similar circumstances), does the behavior occur?" In a previous example, one way to test whether giving (adding) the candy and stopping (subtracting) the crying in the grocery store are, in fact, reinforcers is to think about what would happen if they did not occur after their respective behaviors.

For example, if the child's crying did not stop when the parent gave candy, do you think the parent would continue to give the child candy when the child screams? Probably not. And if the child never got the candy, do you think the child would still scream for it? Again, probably not.

My sister used to call and ask me whether what she did with my niece or nephew was correct or not. My answer was always twofold. First, I would ask her what she wanted them to do. Then I would ask whether they did what she wanted the next time opportunity arose for the behavior to occur again (similar circumstances). I could not tell her whether what she did was right. Only the behavior of my niece or nephew could tell her that. So, in general, if your child is not doing what you want him or her to do, then you're not doing something right. You can always ask the Dr. Phil question about how you're handling your child's behavior: "How's that working for you?"

If You're Gonna Do It, Do It Right!

Reinforcement, like any other scientific discovery, is neither good nor bad, but it can be used for good — to strengthen desirable behavior — or bad — to strengthen undesirable behavior. That's why I call reinforcement an *equal opportunity consequence*.

Some outcomes that may be intended as positive reinforcers really aren't. For example, suppose that when a teenage son takes out the trash when his friends are visiting him his mother immediately gives him a big kiss. Is the kiss a positive reinforcer for taking out the trash? Well, it is *positive* because it is _____ after the behavior of taking out the trash, but it is only a reinforcer if taking out the trash is _____ likely to occur in similar circumstances. But if the behavior doesn't occur more often when his friends are there, then the kiss is just a kiss, or worse, it could actually function as a punisher for taking out the trash if that behavior *decreases* or occurs less often in similar circumstances (see Chapter 7).

On the other hand, some outcomes that may be intended as punishment not only do not work that way (i.e., to decrease the behavior they immediately follow in similar circumstances), they may actually work as positive reinforcement.

Suppose, for example, that a child interrupts his mother when she is on the telephone and she immediately yells, "Don't interrupt me when I'm on the phone!" But the next time she is on the phone he interrupts again. Was her yelling a positive reinforcer? You might say "No, because the yelling is not a positive thing for the child." But remember whether an outcome is considered *positive* depends on whether it is *given* or _____ after the behavior, and NOT whether we feel it is good or like it. In this example, the yelling is <u>added</u>, so it is positive (+). But is it a reinforcer? The answer depends on whether the child's interrupting continues or occurs more often in similar circumstances, that is, the next time the mother is on the phone and he wants her attention. In this case the behavior occurs again, so the mother's yelling is, in fact, a _____ _____*er* for the son's interruptions.

Every day, parents provide a variety of outcomes or consequences, including reprimands and spankings, intended to punish their children's behaviors, only to find that they have to keep reprimanding or spanking their kids. The fact that they continue to do this is often a clue that they may actually be reinforcing (i.e., strengthening) the very behaviors they want to decrease. That is why it is important to look at whether the behavior in question occurs more or less often in similar circumstances.

Consider children who throw tantrums because they immediately get the parent's attention. Some parents yell at their kids, some spank their kids, some try comforting them with hugs and soothing talk, and some try reasoning with their kids. In fact, there are some so-called experts who recommend that when your child throws a tantrum or otherwise loses control, you should put your arms around them and comfort them until they calm down. While this sounds logical and reasonable, it could be the worst thing to do if the behavior of throwing a tantrum increases or continues to occur in the future under similar circumstances. This is because the attention, regardless of what it looks like, may very well be a *positive* _____er for the tantrum, which means that the tantrum is _____ likely to keep occurring. Worse, neither the child nor the parent is having a good time and feeling good about each other or themselves. It is not fun to cry and scream and pull hair and throw objects, and it is not fun to have to hear it every day or find yourself yelling at or hitting your child (see Appendix I for a lengthier discussion of throwing tantrums).

Many of the examples I have used so far illustrate the first of two problems many parents have with positive reinforcement: They (1) <u>inadvertently use positive reinforcement to increase some undesirable behavior</u>, or (2) <u>miss chances to use positive reinforcement to increase some desirable behavior</u>. Throughout the book, I will offer examples of both these errors and try to teach you how to avoid making them.

Remember that whether you know it or not, or like it or not, you always use reinforcement when you interact with your child.

One purpose of this book is to teach you to be aware of how you already use positive (or negative) reinforcement (for good or bad). Another is to teach you how you can change the way you use positive (or negative) reinforcement to improve your child's behavior. If you are successful (and I hope you are), you benefit by having your child behave in more desirable ways. And maybe even more importantly, your child benefits because she is now acting in more desirable ways and getting what she wants. The end result is that everyone is happier and feels better about themselves and they have more positive self-esteem.

Reinforcement and Self-Esteem

The title of this book is *How to Build Good Behavior and Self-Esteem*. I have asserted that using positive reinforcement to increase desirable behavior in your child will automatically improve his or her self-esteem, and, conversely, using negative reinforcement may produce the opposite effect. Let's talk about what self-esteem is and how to change it.

It is important to remember that self-esteem is not a thing that we possess that can be strengthened; it is a label for a set of learned behaviors. Also, self-esteem can't explain behavior. For example, if we say that a child doesn't talk much or make eye contact, because she has low self-esteem, this is a circular explanation if the evidence that the child has low self-esteem is that she doesn't talk much or make eye contact. Self-esteem is a vague concept. Thus, there is no commonly accepted definition, but as you will see below, I will use "self-esteem" to refer to how we talk about ourselves, to others or to ourselves, privately (our so-called "inner voice") — in other words, what we think about ourselves.

Someone with poor self-esteem may repeatedly say that he is a failure or that he can't do something, even in the face of contrary evidence. Such negative self-statements may occur as a response to real or perceived failures and regardless of specific experiences. A person described as having poor self-esteem also may not try new things or may not initiate behaviors such as conversations.

We learn our self-esteem largely from the way our parents talk to and treat us as children. And we often find friends or spouses who talk to and treat us the same way. If we were criticized for particular behaviors, then we probably learned to criticize ourselves.

Another source of poor self-esteem is frequent failure. Children may be set up for it if they are expected to be perfect — an impossible goal in any endeavor — or if they are not taught properly, which may include not receiving positive reinforcement for success. For example, many people are not taught how to do more than simple kinds of math. Consequently, they report having math anxiety or not feeling confident in their math skills. No wonder.

I am using the term *self-esteem* in two related ways. **First, self-esteem refers to how a person thinks about or "sees" herself, that is, *how a person talks to herself about herself*.** For example, a child who is always ridiculed (e.g., "You're so clumsy," or "You really can't do anything right") will begin to talk to herself in similar ways under the same circumstances (i.e., when she bumps into something or stumbles or doesn't succeed at a task). She might even report such observations to others. For example, after accidentally dropping and breaking a glass, she might say to her friends, "I'm such a klutz." On the other hand, a child who is always told that she does things well will say similar things to herself, and maybe to others.

The second meaning of *self-esteem* deals with how we "feel" about ourselves. This meaning is more difficult. Usually when we succeed at something, meaning some behavior is positively reinforced, we feel good about ourselves — we are said to have high self-esteem. Conversely, when we fail at something, meaning the behavior is not positively reinforced, we are said to have low self-esteem.

However, remember the example of the child throwing a tantrum in the grocery store? In that case, the child's tantrum is positively reinforced (by getting candy or the parent's attention). Yet the child doesn't feel good about himself because the behavior of throwing the tantrum is so emotionally upsetting.

So, to increase a child's self-esteem, parents need to do two things: Positively reinforce desirable behavior, usually with attention and approval (hugs and kisses, high fives, etc.), AND talk to your child in approving ways. As we will see, such encouraging talk must be contingent on the child's desirable behavior. That means that such talk should occur ONLY IF the behavior occurs. For example, it is not a good idea to make such general statements to your child as "You're so beautiful," or "You're the best boy in the whole world," or "You're so smart," or "You're a great artist." A better alternative is to say more specific things such as "You really look nice in that dress," or "I really appreciate that you helped your sister set the table," or "You did a great job on your math homework," or "I really like the dinosaur you drew" *immediately after* the desired behavior occurs. Because these statements are contingent on some desirable behavior, and because they are about these specific behaviors, and not about the child, they are more likely to foster self-esteem. In other words, the child is more likely to talk to him- or herself in similar ways.

Just because positively reinforcing statements are dependent on some behavior by the child does not mean that your love for your child is conditional on how the child behaves. But it does mean that your attention and praise should be.

The best rule to follow to increase your child's self-esteem is to: positively reinforce desirable behavior when it occurs and tell your child what you liked about his or her behavior. The self-esteem will follow.

In the next chapter, we look at some of the things you need to know to make positive reinforcement work for you and your children.

Before moving on, try this brief quiz.

Quiz 3

1. Reinforcement is called a *law* because it applies _____ .

2. A *reinforcer* is any usually immediate _____ of a behavior that makes the behavior _____ likely to occur again.

3. There are two kinds of reinforcement: positive and negative. *Positive* simply means that the reinforcer is _____ , as in addition (+). *Negative* means that the reinforcer is _____ , as in subtraction (-).

4. True or False? In most instances, we are aware of how we are reinforcing someone's behavior. _____

5. In order to tell whether some outcome of behavior is a (positive) reinforcer, you must be able to show that the behavior is _____ likely to occur under _____ circumstances.

6. True or False? Positive reinforcement can be used to strengthen good or bad behavior. _____

7. True or False? Negative reinforcement can be used to strengthen good or bad behavior. _____

8. Two positive reinforcement errors many parents commit are inadvertently reinforcing _____ behavior and missing chances to reinforce _____ behavior.

9. Self-esteem refers to how a person both _____ and _____ about herself.

10. In order to increase a child's self-esteem, parents must _____*ly* _____ desirable behavior and talk to the child in _____ ways.

Quiz 3 Answers

1. Reinforcement is called a *law* because it applies *universally.*

2. A *reinforcer* is any usually immediate *outcome (or consequence)* of a behavior that makes the behavior *more* likely to occur again.

3. There are two kinds of reinforcement: positive and negative. *Positive* simply means that the reinforcer is *added*, as in addition (+). *Negative* means that the reinforcer is *subtracted*, as in subtraction (-).

4. True or False? In most instances, we are aware of how we are reinforcing someone's behavior. *False*

5. In order to tell whether some outcome of behavior is a (positive) reinforcer, you must be able to show that the behavior is *more* likely to occur under *similar* circumstances.

6. True or False? Positive reinforcement can be used to strengthen good or bad behavior. *True*

7. True or False? Negative reinforcement can be used to strengthen good or bad behavior. *True*

8. Two positive reinforcement errors many parents commit are inadvertently reinforcing *bad (or undesirable or inappropriate)* behavior or missing chances to reinforce *good (or desirable or appropriate)* behavior.

9. Self-esteem refers to how a person both *thinks* and *feels* about herself.

10. In order to increase a child's self-esteem, parents must *positively reinforce* desirable behavior and talk to the child in *approving (or confirming or supportive)* ways.

Chapter 4: Seven Factors That Make Positive Reinforcement Work

The seven factors that make positive reinforcement work are:

1. Personalization – the reinforcer must fit the particular child.

2. Motivation – the child must want the reinforcer.

3. Timing – the reinforcer must follow behavior immediately.

4. Dependence – the reinforcer must be dependent on the desired behavior.

5. Amount/Effort – the amount of the reinforcer must be big enough and the effort involved in getting it must not be too high.

6. Schedule – reinforcers must occur often enough to maintain behavior.

7. Consistency – reinforcers must occur consistently.

Before learning how to use positive reinforcement to build good behavior and self-esteem in your child, as well as how to solve everyday behavior problems, you need to know what makes positive reinforcement work. In this chapter, I describe seven things you need to know to use positive reinforcement most successfully.

It would be too easy if you could just use what you think is a positive reinforcer and have it work every time. I've heard some parents and teachers say, "I tried positive reinforcement, but it didn't work." My answer to them is, "Then it wasn't positive reinforcement." By definition, positive reinforcement works — it makes behavior _____ likely to occur in similar circumstances. So, what are these parents and teachers doing wrong?

For one, they don't understand that a reinforcer is defined by the fact that it *increases* or *strengthens* behavior in *similar circumstances*. The bottom line is that if you add (or subtract) something after behavior, no matter what you think about it, if the behavior isn't *more* likely to occur again when the next opportunity for it to do so arises, then it wasn't reinforcement. In addition, however, there are several factors that contribute to making something work as a reinforcer, including: 1) Personalization, 2) Motivation, 3) Timing, 4) Dependence, 5) Amount/Effort, 6) Schedule, and 7) Consistency.

1. Personalization

The first thing you need to know about positive reinforcement is that **the reinforcer must fit the particular child** (*personalization*). In most cases, this is not a major obstacle, especially since social positive reinforcement in the form of praise, attention, and approval is pretty much a universally effective and desirable reinforcer.

Generally, the same kinds of positive reinforcers work for most kids. Researchers often classify the types of events that have been shown to work as positive reinforcers into several categories, including *edible* (e.g., food), *tangible* (e.g., toys), *activity/privilege* (e.g., watching TV, playing video games, going to a mall or a concert, etc.), *token* (e.g., gold stars, stickers, points, money, etc.), and *social* (e.g., praise, attention, approval, affection). I discuss these in more detail in the next chapter.

Sometimes it is obvious which events might work as positive reinforcers for a particular child. For example, stickers would probably work for a toddler but not for a teenager, and playing video games would work for your teenager but not for your infant.

In cases that are not so self-evident, you can watch the child and see what she spends her time doing, and then try to arrange that activity as a positive reinforcer. For example, if your daughter spends her time playing baseball but not playing with dolls, then it would probably be a waste of time to let her play with dolls as a reinforcer for cleaning her room. Allowing her to go outside and play baseball (activity reinforcer) immediately following the behavior you want to see is a better bet. Or if your son likes to read, then you can give him extra time reading (activity reinforcer) or allow him to check out more books from the library (tangible reinforcer) immediately after he completes his chores on time or even early.

Other than food, there are three types of events that will work as positive reinforcers for most kids most of the time: social attention, activities, and money (or tokens/points). I focus mostly on social and activity reinforcement throughout the book because of their prevalence in human interactions, especially between parents and children, their ease of use, their cost (They're free!), and their power as a positive reinforcer. However, when kids get a little older, money can be used in part to teach them about its value and how to work for it, and parents can kill two birds with one stone by also teaching them about the money itself and some basic math.

2. Motivation

The second factor that is important when using positive reinforcement is **the child must want the reinforcer** (*motivation*). Motivation simply refers to what a child wants at any given moment. So, in addition to knowing which things might work as a positive reinforcer for a child, you also need to have some idea that the child wants the reinforcer. There are some things, such as attention, certain activities, money, and sweets, that kids almost always want. But the effectiveness of many reinforcers waxes and wanes. For example, with food, sometimes kids are simply not hungry. And no kid wants to engage in certain activities, such as listening to music, playing, watching TV, or even eating, constantly.

Remember that what we call a *positive reinforcer* is given or _____ after a behavior and that behavior is _____ likely to occur under similar circumstances. It's a good bet that if a child hasn't eaten in a while, then you could use food to positively reinforce some behavior that the child may not ordinarily do. Likewise, if an adolescent has no money, you could probably use money to reinforce some behaviors, like doing household chores. The less a child engages in a certain activity, such as building LEGOs, watching TV, reading, or playing outside, the more access to those activities can be used as a reinforcer for engaging in less desirable activities. I will discuss activity reinforcers in more detail in the next chapter. Finally, the less attention a child gets, the more likely attention can be used to positively reinforce some behavior. However, I would never recommend depriving a child of attention in order to use it as a reinforcer. I will discuss how to use attention as a reinforcer in the next chapter.

But She's Not Motivated

Using positive reinforcement also solves the problem of low or poor motivation. What do I mean by "low or poor motivation"?

Many kids often do not behave as we would want or like them to. Sometimes, especially in school settings, we say that kids who do not perform as we would like them to have no or low motivation. However, as you learned in Chapter 2, explaining behavior as being caused by low motivation is an example of a type of faulty explanation called a circular explanation.

Remember that in a circular explanation, *the evidence for the explanation is the very behavior you want to explain*. In the case of low or poor motivation, the only way parents or teachers could ever know that a child has low or poor motivation is by her behavior. If she doesn't participate in class, doesn't do her schoolwork, doesn't answer questions addressed to her, etc., we might conclude that she isn't motivated. But in such cases, low or poor motivation is just a name for not doing the work or not answering questions. A child who does her work and who answers questions is said to be highly motivated.

It is common to blame such children for not being motivated and to throw up our hands. But let's look at it from a different perspective: It is not a problem of low motivation, but a problem of a lack of positive reinforcement for the very behaviors that the child does not engage in.

A child who doesn't participate in a classroom also doesn't have the opportunity to receive positive reinforcement for appropriate behavior. All too often, such children end up sitting in the back, which makes it even more difficult to participate. Teachers (and parents) can blame it on low motivation and give up their responsibility for the child, or they can arrange for the child to behave in ways that can earn positive reinforcement.

In general, when a kid doesn't exhibit much behavior to positively reinforce, a parent or teacher must arrange it so that she can engage in some simple behaviors that the parent or teacher can then positively reinforce. There are many ways to accomplish this.

One way is to look for any appropriate behavior, no matter how small, and reinforce it. For example, suppose the child did raise her hand or said an answer out loud, even if incorrect. The teacher should then praise her for that, perhaps by saying, "Vivi, that's a good try." Or a teacher could ask the student a simple question that the student knows the answer to and then praise her for answering it.

In general, you can increase a child's motivation by increasing the frequency and amount of reinforcement for behaviors which show motivation.

3. Timing Is Everything

In Chapter 3, you learned that a reinforcer is *any outcome of a behavior that makes the behavior more likely to happen again in similar circumstances.* **The general rule is: The more immediately a positive reinforcer follows a behavior, the stronger the effect it has.**

This rule should make common sense to you. For example, suppose you ask your 3-year-old to pick up a book and he does so, but you don't praise him until an hour later. Do you think the praise would reinforce picking up the book? Why not? (You're right if you said that the child would have forgotten why he was praised!) With older kids, delayed reinforcement might work, but no matter the age it's best to always give reinforcement as

_____ after the desired behavior as possible. And by "immediately" I mean within 1 or 2 seconds of the desired behavior!

As kids get older, we can praise them much later after a behavior and that might still increase their tendency to engage in the behavior. We probably don't want to call it reinforcement, however, because it works differently. When you praise an older kid, even if it is long after some behavior, they're likely to immediately repeat the praise, even if only to themselves. The next time they engage in the behavior, they may, in fact, praise themselves (usually silently to themselves) like you did on the previous occasion.

4. You Can Depend on It

The general rule about dependence is: The more a reinforcer is dependent on a behavior, the stronger effect it will have. A reinforcer is dependent on a behavior if it occurs <u>only</u> after that behavior and for no other behavior. Again, this makes sense if you think about it. For example, suppose a parent tells a child, "You have to eat your vegetables if you want dessert" (Grandma's Rule). After not eating the vegetables, the child pleads with the parent to let him have some dessert anyway, and the parent gives in. In this example, the reinforcer of getting the _____ occurs immediately after pleading; that is, it is dependent not on eating vegetables, but on _____. It is no wonder why the child won't eat his vegetables and why he will learn to plead in similar situations. To repeat, reinforcers should occur if and *only* if the desired _____ occurs.

5. Amount/Effort

Additional factors that influence the effectiveness of positive reinforcement are the *amount* of the reinforcer given and, relatedly, the *effort* a response involves. **The general rule is: The greater the amount of a reinforcer and the less effortful the response, the more effective the reinforcer**. For example, giving your child $1 for mowing the yard may not increase yard-mowing because the reinforcer amount is too low relative to the effort of the response. If what you want your child to do requires a lot of effort, then you should increase the _____ of the reinforcer. Alternatively, you could break the behavior up into smaller segments and reinforce the completion of each one with a smaller reinforcer. Such a tactic would work well with piano practice, or doing homework, or even cleaning a messy room. So, remember, your child is more likely to do what you want if the effort in doing so is relatively _____ and the amount of the reward is relatively _____. If you said "low" and "large" respectively, you're right!

6. Schedule

Once a friend told me about how his dog would always jump up on him and on strangers. I asked him what he did right after the dog jumped up. He said, "Sometimes I push him down and tell him 'No!'" I replied, "Well, you must be reinforcing the jumping by pushing the dog down and saying no." "But" my friend said, "I hardly ever do that." He was implying that because he rarely pushed the dog down, he couldn't have been reinforcing the jumping. I've heard similar stories from parents who sometimes say that because they hardly ever pay attention to crying or complaining, they can't be reinforcing the behavior.

These stories illustrate a fifth factor that affects the success of positive reinforcement: the schedule with which reinforcement is delivered. Behavioral scientists have discovered several such schedules in the laboratory, but for the present purposes, I will focus on two.

The first type of schedule is called a *continuous reinforcement schedule* (CRF), which means each instance of a behavior (each response) is followed by a reinforcer.

Let's turn the previous example on its head and suppose that you wanted to teach your dog to jump up on you. How would you do that? Well, first you would have to identify what you could use as a reinforcer. Usually, when training a dog, we use bits of food coupled with praise, but in this example, we'll just use praise. So, every time the dog jumps on you, you would say "Good dog!"

In other words, the schedule would be a _____ _____ schedule or __ __ __ for short.

    You would use the same CRF schedule in the beginning of teaching anything to anyone. For example, if you want to teach your child to name her colors, in the beginning you would say "Good!" every time she calls a red object "red" and a green object "green," etc. Or if you want to teach your son to remove his dishes from the table, you would praise him every time he removes a dish in the beginning.

    After a while in both examples, you would eventually stop praising the response every time and begin to praise every other time, then every third time, and then sporadically. And guess what? Not only will the behavior continue, it will actually become stronger. It will persist in the absence of your praise. This is the second type of reinforcement schedule. It's called an *intermittent reinforcement schedule*, which means that the reinforcer doesn't occur for every response but only for some responses.

    Consider what happens when you call your child to come to you. Sometimes she answers after you call her once, but other times she only answers after you call her two, three, or four times, or even more. So even though your child doesn't answer you every time you call her, you still continue to call her. Your behavior of calling her is thus being reinforced on an _____ schedule.

    Intermittent reinforcement generates very persistent behavior, which means it continues to occur in the absence of obvious reinforcement. So, when someone tells me that they hardly ever reinforce, or pay attention to, some behavior, the "hardly ever" tells me that they are actually using an _____ schedule. Now that's a good thing if the behavior is desirable.

    When I was growing up, my parents used to say, "If you don't succeed, try, try again." What they were trying to tell me, even if they didn't know it, was that behavior is often on an intermittent reinforcement schedule and reinforcement will eventually come if I keep behaving (trying). We want to teach our kids to persist and not to give up in the face of failure. The best way to prepare them for that is to reinforce their behavior on a continuous schedule in the beginning of teaching and then gradually move it to an intermittent reinforcement schedule.

Of course, bad behavior, too, is often reinforced intermittently, which is why it's so hard to get rid of it.

A general rule about reinforcement schedules is: The more intermittent the reinforcement, the more persistent the behavior.

7. Consistency

A final factor that affects the success of positive reinforcement — and, indeed, everything I discuss in this book — is consistency. Consistency is related to dependence. It means that if you've decided to positively reinforce some behavior, you should do so consistently.

For example, suppose you want to encourage your teenager to talk to you, but he does so at an inconvenient time, and you tell him you are busy. You probably won't reinforce the behavior and he won't try to talk to you in the future. Not only do you miss a chance to positively reinforce the very behavior you want, but you might inadvertently punish (i.e., decrease) or discourage the behavior (see Chapter 7). There are exceptions to this rule, however, which I will discuss later in the book.

In addition to problems of consistency with one parent, there are often problems of consistency between two parents or different adults. For example, it is well known that if a child can't get when he wants from one parent, he will often approach the other parent. Why? Remember that reinforcement is defined as a consequence of behavior that makes that behavior _____ likely to occur in similar circumstances. In this case, the similar circumstance is the parent who will give in to the child's demand, thus reinforcing his request. If the parents are on the same page (they have discussed what to do under these circumstances), and neither parent gives in, the child will stop asking. **The general rule is: The more consistently both parents act toward their children, the more consistently the children will act.**

Before going on, try this brief quiz.

Quiz 4

1. A particular reinforcer must _____ a particular person, and, relatedly, the person must _____ the reinforcer.

2. True or False? Generally, the same kinds of positive reinforcers work for most people. _____

3. True or False? It is NOT possible to determine ahead of time what things might work as positive reinforcers for a particular individual. _____

4. The three types of things that will work as positive reinforcers for most people are social _____, _____, and _____.

5. The general rule about the timing of reinforcers is: The more _____ a positive reinforcer follows some behavior, the stronger the effect it has.

6. The _____ dependent a reinforcer is on a particular behavior, the stronger effect it will have.

7. The _____ the amount of reinforcement and the _____ effortful the response, the more effective the reinforcer.

8. Another factor that affects the success of positive reinforcement is whether the reinforcer follows the behavior most of the time — a rule called _____.

9. A fifth factor that affects the success of positive reinforcement is the schedule with which reinforcement is delivered. There are two types of schedules: one in which every response is reinforced,

called _____, and one in which not every response is reinforced, called _____.

10. A child who is said to not be motivated is simply not receiving enough positive _____ for behaving.

Quiz 4 Answers

1. A particular reinforcer must *fit* a particular person, and, relatedly, the person must *want* the reinforcer.

2. True or False? Generally, the same kinds of positive reinforcers work for most people. *True*

3. True or False? It is NOT possible to determine ahead of time what things might work as positive reinforcers for a particular individual. *False*

4. The three types of events that will work as positive reinforcers for most people are social *attention, activities,* and *money/tokens.*

5. The general rule about the timing of reinforcers is: The more *immediately* a positive reinforcer follows some behavior, the stronger the effect it has.

6. The *more* dependent a reinforcer is on a particular behavior, the stronger effect it will have.

7. The *greater* the amount of reinforcement and the *less* effortful the response, the more effective the reinforcer.

8. Another factor that affects the success of positive reinforcement is whether the reinforcer follows the behavior most of the time — a rule called *consistency.*

9. A fifth factor that affects the success of positive reinforcement is the schedule with which reinforcement is delivered. There are two types of schedules: one in which every response is reinforced, called *continuous,* and one in which not every response is reinforced, called *intermittent.*

10. A child who is said to not be motivated is simply not receiving enough positive *reinforcement* for behaving.

Chapter 5: Five Types of Positive Reinforcers

The five types of positive reinforcers are:

1. Edible – different types of foods.

2. Tangible –toys and other objects.

3. Activity/privilege – activities, like playing video games, etc.

4. Token –things like money and can be in the form of poker chips, gold stars, points, etc.

5. Social – attention, praise, and approval.

At the beginning of Chapter 4, I listed five types of positive reinforcers: *edible, tangible, activity/privilege, token,* and *social* reinforcers. In this chapter, I describe the first four of these in slightly more detail, followed by a lengthier description of social reinforcement.

1. Edible Reinforcers

This one is easy. Food will often work as a positive reinforcer. And many types of foods, such as candy, sweets, or chips (which I do not recommend using for obvious reasons), will work as positive reinforcers even when the child is not hungry. Edible reinforcers are often used in the beginning stages when teaching children diagnosed with autism or other disabilities. With other kids, however, they should probably only be used when other reinforcers won't work, or when they make logical sense, such as allowing a child to eat dessert, or some other food she likes, only if she eats her vegetables (Grandma's Rule), or when used in small quantities. For example, you can occasionally use a special dessert or treat if a child has a really good piano practice or does a great job with her homework or cleaning her room, especially if she initiates any of these activities.

2. Tangible Reinforcers

Tangible reinforcers include any object you can give a child, such as toys, books, LEGOs, games, videos, etc. Parents frequently give their children things, but rarely, if ever, are the things contingent on some specific desired behavior. It is up to you whether you want to give objects to your children dependent on some behavior, but doing so may teach them to be more responsible, because as adults we usually have to work to get things.

Also, undesirable behaviors such as whining, complaining, throwing tantrums, fighting with siblings, etc., often result in getting things, which reinforces those behaviors, meaning they are more _____ to occur in similar circumstances.

For example, before parents have taught such self-control behaviors as waiting, very young children will whine or cry or pout when they don't get something they want or when parents take something away. It would be a mistake, however, for the parents to give the child what he wants under such circumstances because that will teach the child to _____, _____, or _____ under similar circumstances. Not giving in when these behaviors occur will frequently make the behaviors worse in the short term, a problem we will deal with in Chapter 6. Alternatively, you may want to consider only allowing access to tangible items contingent on NOT engaging in these behaviors and doing something else, such as behaviors that result in waiting.

3. Token Reinforcers

Token reinforcers include anything (e.g., poker chips, points, gold stars, etc.) that can be traded in or exchanged at a later time for other reinforcers, called *back-up reinforcers*, such as tangible, edible, or activity reinforcers.

For example, parents might post a chart on the refrigerator or on the door of the child's room and give a point to their 10-year-old son every time he takes his dishes off the table after a meal. At the end of the week, if he earns enough points, he may exchange them for other things such as a video, a trip to the skate park, or a new book.

The types of tokens that you use and when the child can exchange them depend, in part, on the age of the child. For example, stickers or gold stars might work better for very young children who don't understand what points are yet. Because of their age, it is probably best to allow these children to exchange the gold stars fairly soon after the end of a particular activity. If you decide to use points for an older child, they will need to be exchanged for some other more potent reinforcer such as an object (a LEGO set) or, better yet, access to an activity (e.g., playing outside, watching a video, etc.). The younger the child the sooner they should be able to exchange the tokens or points, for example after they do the behavior you want, but probably no later than the end of the day. For older kids, they can probably wait until the end of a week or longer. However, the tokens themselves must always be given immediately and contingently on the desired behavior. Remember, everything you try is an experiment, so if something doesn't work, don't keep doing it. Change it and try again.

For families of multiple children, a token system is a good way to get all the kids on the same page. In such cases, there are at least three ways you can administer a token system with more than one child.

1. In an *independent group contingency*, all children are required to do some behavior, such as make their beds or do other chores in order to earn a token, but only those kids who actually do the behavior get a token. In other words, each child is *independent* of his or her siblings. This one is the most difficult for parents to carry out because parents have to keep track of each child's progress, and also because when parents give a token to one child and not another, the one who didn't get the token may protest, which demands that the parents have a plan for that behavior (see Chapter 6).

2. In an *interdependent group contingency*, all of the kids must meet the goal for all of them to earn a token. So, whether any one kid earns a token depends on all of his or her siblings meeting their goal. This one is the easiest for parents to carry out because they don't have to treat each kid differently. Also, with the *interdependent group contingency*, each kid can act to encourage his or her siblings to meet the goal. That means that the parent doesn't have to remind or nag them and the children learn to cooperate with one another.

3. In a *dependent group contingency*, all of the kids earn a token if one of them meets the goal, meaning that whether the group earns a token depends on one child meeting his or her goal. This one is also relatively easy to carry out because the parents only need to keep track of one kid. However, in this case, not all of the kids are required to do the behavior, which can be a problem if the parents want them all to do it.

Research has shown that all three types of group token economies are effective with the interdependent contingency being slightly more effective. However, you can try each one to see which one works best for your family. Remember that experimentation is the only way to know what works.

Incidentally, things like stickers or gold stars might sometimes work as positive reinforcers for very young children without being exchanged for other reinforcers, which would make them tangible automatic reinforcers. It is possible, or even likely, that stickers or gold stars work because they are novel. But the novelty will likely wear off, so it's a good idea to have some back-up reinforcers available.

4. Activity/Privilege Reinforcers

One of the most powerful types of (positive) reinforcement is the opportunity to engage in certain behaviors or activities. There are always activities that children (and adults) want to engage in. Put more simply, there are always things we want to do.

On the other hand, there are always things we have to do. This is the essence of what we refer to as **self-control**: *doing what we have to do before doing what we want to do*. Many successful people have self-control in that they put off doing what they want until they do what they need to do.

Decades of research have shown that the activities a child likes to engage in (e.g., playing video games, talking on the telephone, texting, social networking, watching TV, drawing, playing outside, etc.) can be used as reinforcers for activities the child may not like to engage in (e.g., washing the dishes, studying, taking the trash out, etc.). This phenomenon is referred to as *Grandma's Rule* (also known as the Premack Principle, named after the researcher who first studied it): *the opportunity to engage in a more desirable activity can reinforce doing a less desirable activity*. Grandma's Rule takes the form of "If, then" statements: "*If* you want to do Y, *then* you have to do X." Or, **if you do the less desirable activity first, then, <u>and only then</u>, you may engage in the more desirable activity**.

Parents can begin to use Grandma's Rule with young infants with very simple behaviors. For example, when our son was 18 months old, we began saying things like, "If you take one more bite of oatmeal, you can get down (out of the highchair)," or "You can watch TV if you pick up your toys." In fact, we were always aware of what he wanted to do and what we wanted him to do and mostly allowed him to do what he wanted if he did what we wanted him to do. He is 10 now, and we still use Grandma's Rule more than anything else except for praise and attention. Moreover, he now exhibits better self-control than some adults. Without us saying anything, he will put off doing the things he likes to do until he has engaged in less desirable behaviors.

As children get older, there are more and more things they have to do to become independent — one of the main goals of parenting. Because there are always things kids want to do, you can never run out of ways to use Grandma's Rule. Here are a few examples:

- *If* you finish your dinner, *then* you can watch the video.

- *If* you clean off the table, *then* you can play in your room.
- *If* you finish one page of your homework, *then* you can draw.
- *If* you practice your piano for 15 minutes, *then* you can go outside and ride your scooter.

Because kids are typically on a different schedule than adults, you may also include a time limit for these rules, such as "*If* you finish your dinner *before* the timer times out, *then* you can watch the video." Or "If you clean off the table in less than 5 minutes, you can play for 10 minutes" (see Appendix I for a discussion of using a timer).

Other than social reinforcers (see below), the most effective positive reinforcers to use are activity/privilege reinforcers, which, as mentioned above, also serve very effectively as back-up reinforcers in a token system.

Activity reinforcers include activities that children would normally do on their own without reinforcement from others. You might say these activities are "intrinsically reinforcing," which means only that doing the activity itself is its own reinforcer (see Appendix II for a brief discussion of intrinsic vs. extrinsic reinforcement). For example, listening to music and playing basketball may be their own reinforcers in the sense that no one else has to provide rewards for children to engage in them.

To reiterate, Grandma's Rule states that a behavior a person engages in frequently can be used to positively reinforce a behavior that person doesn't engage in much. For example, listening to music can be used to positively reinforce cleaning one's room, or playing basketball can be used to positively reinforce doing homework. Of course, the parent must follow the rules for what makes reinforcement work by allowing the child to listen to music or play basketball *if and only if* he cleans his room or does homework (dependency) and immediately after those behaviors (timing). To determine which activity/privilege will work as a positive reinforcer, all the parent needs to do is observe what the child normally does and then make access to that behavior dependent on the behavior the parent desires. **It is**

important to remember that if your child fails to do the desired behavior, you do not allow him/her access to the preferred activity.

5. Social Reinforcers

So far, I have described *edible, tangible, token,* and *activity/privilege* reinforcers. As I stated in Chapter 4, the two most powerful reinforcers are activity/privilege and social reinforcers for very similar reasons: they're free, easy to use, powerful, and in great abundance. However, because we are social beings, social reinforcers are not in short supply. Social reinforcers are implied in the concepts of *attention, approval, or affection.*

Attention can include someone looking at or listening to you, nodding, smiling, talking to you, and, of course, using praise, which would suggest approval, or affection such as hugs and kisses. A large majority of our interactions with others involve talking (speaking, signing, writing), and in order for someone to listen to you, you have to have his or her attention (e.g., eye contact, etc.). Imagine how little contact with other people you would have in a given day if you didn't talk to them. That is why the most important form of attention parents can give children is in the form of talking.

Two Ways of Talking as Social Positive Reinforcement: There are basically two ways that you can use talking as a social positive reinforcer for children's behavior. First, simply talking to them while they are behaving in appropriate ways can positively reinforce those behaviors. Of course, talking to kids when they are misbehaving often reinforces the misbehavior (see Appendix I for a discussion of answering everything a child says).

Consider, for example, a situation in which a parent and a child go into a store and the child is walking by the parent's side and behaving well. If the parent would just talk to the child — about anything — and respond to the child's talking, that normal interaction would probably reinforce the child's desirable behavior and, equally important, prevent any undesirable behavior from occurring.

Unfortunately, parents often (unintentionally) ignore the child's desirable behaviors in these circumstances because they are busy. If asked, they might report that they are happy their child is being quiet and not causing a commotion. But as soon as the child misbehaves, the parent immediately talks to her by saying such things as "Stop that," "Be quiet," or "I told you not to take things off the shelves," etc. Often, and unbeknownst to the parent, saying (adding) these things to the child right after the child misbehaves may _____*ly*_____ the child's misbehavior so that the behavior is more likely to occur again in similar circumstances. This is especially likely if the child is not getting much attention for desirable behaviors.

A second way that you can use talking to children as a positive social reinforcer is to show your approval by using *specific* (or directed) *praise*. **Specific praise** is just what its name implies: **you praise the *specific* behavior (instead of the person) at the time it occurs**. Often, I hear parents saying things like "You're such a good boy," or "You're the best little girl in the whole world," or "You're so cute!" or "You're a great artist!" However, a more honest and effective way to praise is to say something like, "Thank you for doing what I asked," or "I really like the way you folded those clothes and put them in the drawer," or "Thanks for saying 'please'" or "I like how you blended those colors in your painting." In each of these cases, the specific behavior has been praised.

Specific praise serves two functions. First, it tells the child exactly what she did that you like, so she'll know the next time. And second, it may positively reinforce the behavior, which means that the behavior is _____ likely to occur under similar circumstances.

To get some practice, provide specific praise for the behaviors in the following examples.

- A parent asks an 8-year-old child to remove dishes from the dinner table and put them in the sink. When the child does so, the parent immediately says "_____
_____."

- A 6-year-old is in her room reading quietly while the parents have visitors. As soon as the visitors leave, the parents go to the child's room and say "_____ _____."

- A 5-year-old sister helps her 2-year-old brother brush his teeth. The parent immediately says to the girl, "_____ _____."

In the first example, you might have said, "I like the way you took the dishes off the table and put them in the sink," or "Thank you for taking the dishes off the table and putting them in the sink." In the second example, you might have said, "Thanks for playing or reading by yourself when our friends were visiting." And in the third example, you might have said, "I really like the way you helped your brother brush his teeth," or "You're a grown-up girl for helping your brother brush his teeth."

Also, using specific praise is mostly useful in the beginning stages of getting a child to do something, when you're using a continuous schedule of reinforcement. Once the child learns to comply with your request and does so often and without incident, you probably do not need to use specific praise, or do not need to use it every time (intermittent schedule). But you can always hold it in reserve for new tasks or for those that are difficult to complete.

It turns out that attention, mostly talking, is the most often used and the most powerful type of positive reinforcement. Unfortunately, as I have already indicated, it is often given (added) unintentionally for undesirable behaviors. In the following examples, try to answer what the social positive reinforcer is and what behavior is being reinforced (strengthened).

- Parents put a toddler to bed and leave the room. The child starts to cry and scream "let me out." After a few minutes, the parents go back into the room and try to comfort and reassure the child by saying, "We're right outside if you need us." *If* the child is more likely to cry and scream and say similar things when put to bed, then...

1. The positive reinforcer in this example is the parents'

_____.

2. The behavior that is reinforced is the child's _____

_____.

You're right if you said that the positive reinforcer is the parents going back into the room and comforting and telling their child "We're right outside if you need us." And the behavior they likely reinforced was crying and screaming.

- An 8-year-old calls her father from the other side of the house to "Come help me now!" So, the father says "OK," stops washing the dishes, and goes to his daughter. *If* she is more likely to call him from the other side of the house, then…

1. The positive reinforcer in this example is the father's

_____.

2. The behavior that is reinforced is the child's _____

_____.

You're right if you said that the positive reinforcer is the father going to his daughter when she calls to him from the other side of the house, and her behavior of demanding that he help her is reinforced.

- A 3-year-old comes home from preschool and utters a bad word, and even though it causes the parents to chuckle, they immediately sit her down and explain why such words are not appropriate. Now they notice that their daughter says such words often, and no matter how much they tell her these words are unacceptable, she continues to use them.

1. The positive reinforcer in this example is the parents'

_____.

2. The behavior that is reinforced is the child's _____

_____.

You're right if you said that the positive reinforcer is the parents' chuckling and explaining to their daughter why such words are not appropriate and that her behavior of saying such words has been reinforced.

- An 8-year-old complains that he doesn't want to do his chores. When the parent tells him that he has to, the boy once again complains and whines. He asks why he has to do it, and the parent explains why it is important to do chores. *If* he is more likely to complain and whine when his parents tell him to do his chores, then...
  1. The positive reinforcer in this example is _____
  _____.
  2. The behavior that is reinforced is _____
  _____.

You're right if you said that the positive reinforcer is the parent's talking to and answering the child and the behavior that is reinforced is the son's continued complaining and asking.

- A 4-year-old screams and cries and hits the parent when he doesn't get his way. The parent hugs and comforts him until he calms down. *If* he is more likely to scream and cry when he doesn't get his way, then...
  1. The positive reinforcer in this example is the parent's
  _____.
  2. The behavior that is reinforced is the child's _____
  _____.

You're right if you said that the positive reinforcer is the parent's hugging and comforting the child and the behavior that is reinforced is the child's screaming and crying and hitting.

In all of these examples, some undesirable behavior is inadvertently positively reinforced by the parents' attention, mostly in the form of talking. What this means is that each of these behaviors is _____ likely to occur under similar _____.

Also, notice that I put the word *If* in italics. This is because we don't know for sure if the behavior will increase under similar circumstances. Remember, we can't tell if something is a reinforcer until we observe an increase in the behavior under similar circumstances. In the next chapter, we will look at ways that each of the parents could have behaved differently.

Of course, simply interacting with and talking to one's children also reinforces good behavior. In Chapter 1, I cited two examples of mothers who were talking to their children when they were behaving appropriately in a public place. I speculated that such attention would probably reinforce the children's behaviors. Many parents interact with their children when they are behaving as the parents would like. Unfortunately, many of the same parents also talk with their children when they are not behaving as the parents would like. So, there is no real dependency between how the children behave and the attention they receive. That means that the kids get attention whether they behave well or not. Imagine what would happen if the children only, or mostly, got attention for behaving well and not behaving badly. I think that by now you know that the children would mostly behave well and would rarely behave badly.

Style and Delivery

Finally, not only is it important to talk to your kids when they are behaving as you would like and to praise specific behaviors that you like and want to see more of, but the style and delivery of what you say can be important. In other words, what you say must be tailored to the specific child, not only for their age and whether they are a boy or girl, but their specific likes and dislikes and traits they may possess.

For example, if you are dealing with a typical adolescent boy, you might want to appeal to his macho view of himself when he does some physical chore by saying something like "Wow! You're really strong." Or when you find your adolescent daughter reading instead of texting on her phone, you can say something like "I'm really glad to see you reading. That's going to make you even smarter than you already are." Or when your 6-year-old son does his chore quickly, you can say something like, "Wow, you are really fast!" Or when your preteen daughter kicks the soccer ball really well, you can say, "Wow, great kick! You looked just like a professional!"

One final word about using social attention. Depending on the child and the behavior, many parents use high-fives or clapping or cheering, all of which constitute social attention, but in a more excited form. Don't be shy about using these things especially for very young children. Also, you might want to save them for more important behaviors or behaviors that are difficult, complex, or last a longer time.

Before moving on, try this brief quiz.

Quiz 5

1. Reinforcers that involve food are called _____ reinforcers.

2. Gold stars, points, or money are types of _____ reinforcers.

3. Reinforcers that involve allowing a child to go out and play or to watch TV are called _____ reinforcers.

4. The rule that states that if you do the less desirable activity first, then, *and only then*, you may engage in the more desirable activity is called _____'s rule.

5. Reinforcers that involve giving things to kids for desirable behavior are called _____ positive reinforcers.

6. Reinforcers that come from interacting with others are called _____ positive reinforcers.

7. In addition to simply talking to others, the other way talking can be used as a positive reinforcer is to target the behavior by using _____ or directed praise.

8. Social and activity reinforcers are preferable to edible and token reinforcers most of the time because they are _____ and _____ to use.

9. Social positive reinforcers are desirable because they are how people, including parents and their children, _____ with each other normally.

10. In addition to talking to your kids and praising specific behaviors that you like and want to see more of, the _____ and _____ of what you say can be important.

Quiz 5 Answers

1. Reinforcers that involve food are called *edible* reinforcers.

2. Gold stars, points, or money are types of *token* reinforcers.

3. Reinforcers that involve allowing a child to go out and play or to watch TV are called *activity* reinforcers.

4. The rule that states that if you do the less desirable activity first, then, *and only then*, you may engage in the more desirable activity is called *Grandma's* Rule.

5. Reinforcers that involve giving things to kids, such as toys, for desirable behavior are called *tangible* positive reinforcers.

6. Reinforcers that come from interacting with others are called *social* positive reinforcers.

7. In addition to simply talking to others, the other way talking can be used as a positive reinforcer is to target the behavior by using *specific* or directed praise.

8. Social and activity reinforcers are preferable to edible and token reinforcers most of the time because they are *free* and *easy* to use.

9. Social positive reinforcers are desirable because they are how people, including parents and their children, *interact* with each other normally.

10. In addition to talking to your kids and praising specific behaviors that you like and want to see more of, the *style* and *delivery* of what you say can be important.

Part III – How to Undo the Effects of Reinforcement on Undesirable Behavior

Chapter 6: Withholding Reinforcement

As mentioned in the last chapter, one of the two mistakes parents frequently make is to unknowingly reinforce a child's undesirable behavior. Once this is done, parents often wonder whether they can then stop the behavior. Many parents intuitively realize and understand that they have something to do with the child behaving inappropriately. Some also realize that they need to stop doing whatever it is they are doing.

Before giving some examples, let me remind you that just as the kid is always right, in the sense that his or her behavior is caused (or determined) by his or her environment, so, too, are the parents always right, in the sense that their behavior is caused by their upbringing and environment. In other words, they do with their kids what they learned from their parents. These behaviors are passed down from generation to generation until a parent begins to think about what they're doing and why.

Now, let me give you an example of a common parenting mistake. A 16-month-old girl would throw things from her highchair when she didn't get something she wanted. The parents (and grandparents) would immediately explain to her why she shouldn't throw things — remember that she was 16 months old! — and then go and pick them up for her. The girl would always throw them again. The aunt, who was a student in my class, figured out that the parents talking to her niece and picking up the things she had thrown might be somehow encouraging (i.e., reinforcing) her behavior. So, she had them all ignore the throwing behavior the next time it happened. However, when they ignored her behavior the next time, the behavior got immediately worse. The little girl began banging her head against the wall, which the parents obviously could not ignore.

What parents often report after such interactions is that they tried to ignore the behavior, but the behavior got worse, and, as we will see, they're right — sort of.

Using Planned Ignoring

As many parents intuitively conclude, the simplest thing to do with undesirable behavior that is reinforced with attention is not to pay attention to the behavior. In fact, this is often the best advice *under certain circumstances*. **The name for NOT giving, or withholding, positive social reinforcement — attention — is** *planned ignoring*. It is called *planned* ignoring because you must *plan* for when and how behaviors can be *ignored*.

Before I describe what happens when you use planned ignoring, try to answer the following questions about the examples from the previous chapter:

1. Parents put a toddler to bed and leave the room. The child starts to cry and to scream "let me out!" After a few minutes, the parents go back into the room and try to comfort and reassure her by saying, "We're right outside if you need us." Instead of the parents going back into the child's room and trying to comfort and reassure her when she cries and screams, the parents could have

   _____.

2. An 8-year-old calls her father from the other side of the house to "Come help me now!" so the father says "OK," stops washing the dishes, and goes to his daughter. Instead of the father going to his daughter when she yells at him to "Come help me now!" he could have

   _____   _____.

3. A 3-year-old comes home from preschool and utters a bad word. Even though it causes the parents to chuckle, they immediately sit her down and explain why such words are not appropriate. Now they notice that their daughter says such words often, and no matter how much they tell her these words are unacceptable, she continues to use them. Instead of the parents chuckling and immediately sitting

their 3-year-old down and explaining to her why swear words are not appropriate, they could have _____

_____.

4. An 8-year-old complains that he doesn't want to do his chores. The parent tells him that he has to. The boy once again complains and whines. He asks why he has to do it, and the parent answers him. Now his parents notice that whenever they ask him to do his chores, or anything for that matter, he complains and whines. Instead of his parents answering him when he asks why he has to do his chores, they could have _____

_____.

5. A 4-year-old screams and cries and hits the parent when he doesn't get his way. The parent hugs and comforts him until he calms down. As a result, he is more likely to scream and cry when he doesn't get his way. Instead of hugging and comforting him when he screams and cries, the parent could have _____

_____.

If your answers to all of the above involved ignoring the kid's behavior, that is, not making any response to the undesirable behavior, you'd be correct. But what does it mean to use planned ignoring and to truly ignore a behavior?

The planned part of *planned ignoring* means that the ignoring should be thought-out ahead of time — *planned* — which means that once you have identified an undesirable behavior, you *plan* when and how you will ignore it. The planning must involve all of the adults (including grandparents, aunts, and uncles), and maybe even other siblings, who interact with the child and are in a position to inadvertently pay attention to the undesirable behavior. That way no one has to make a split-second decision and possibly be caught off-guard.

How do you ignore a behavior? First, **it is important to remember that you are NOT ignoring the child, just a behavior**. Having said that, let's look at how this could be done in the examples above.

1. Instead of the parents going back into the child's room, they could have not gone back into the room (assuming that they had previously made sure their daughter was not hungry, in pain, etc.) and not answered or talked to her.
2. Instead of the father saying "OK" and going to his daughter, he could have said nothing and not stopped washing the dishes and not gone to help his daughter.
3. Instead of the parents chuckling and explaining to her why such words are not appropriate, they could have not chuckled (hard as it might be) and not looked at or said anything to her.
4. Instead of answering their son, the parents could not have answered the child except maybe once by repeating "Please do your chores now."
5. Instead of hugging and comforting the 4-year-old, the parent could have not hugged and tried to comfort him and not looked at or talked to him.

As these examples indicate, **planned ignoring is the opposite of using positive social reinforcement**: Instead of *giving* or *adding* attention after a behavior, you are *withholding* or not giving it. However, I must warn you about a few things to watch out for.

Warning No. 1
Before you use planned ignoring, you should be aware of something very important. **When you withhold a positive social reinforcer after a behavior, there will likely be a burst of the behavior in which it will almost always immediately get worse.** It's as if the person tries harder and harder to get the attention. This is the reason that many parents who try to ignore undesirable behavior say, "I tried to ignore it, but it didn't work." What they mean is that when they ignored the behavior, it got worse (and they gave in). (We'll talk later about why parents give in.)

Warning No. 2

It is NOT advisable to use planned ignoring for behaviors that are already dangerous and destructive. The reason is that when you ignore these behaviors, the immediate burst will result in even more dangerous and destructive behaviors that you won't be able to ignore and that might cause harm to the child or to others. Then when you attend to the more dangerous and destructive behaviors, you will inadvertently reinforce them. (We will deal with examples of behaviors that raise special concerns in Chapter 11.)

Let me illustrate the burst problem with another example. Suppose you put money in a vending machine to get a soda. After you insert your money, you push the appropriate button, but the soda doesn't come rolling out. What do you do? Do you just walk away? I doubt it. What you probably do is press the button again, and then hit the button, and depending on your experience with faulty vending machines, you may actually kick the machine or shake it. Why? You're not normally an aggressive person. The answer is because sometime in the past when you have hit or shaken the machine, the soda came out. Getting the soda, then, is a _____ *reinforcer* for the behavior of _____ the machine.

Now, try to say what each of the children in our examples might do when their social positive reinforcers are withheld:

1. When parents ignore their toddler's crying and screaming ("let me out!") behavior at bedtime, the child might immediately _____
   _____.

2. When the father ignores his 8-year old's calls from the other side of the house to "Come help me now!" the girl might immediately _____
   _____.

3. When the parents ignore their 3-year-old's bad language, she might immediately _____
   _____.

4. When the parent doesn't answer the child, the child's asking and complaining might _____ _____.

5. When the parents withhold the hugs and don't look at or talk to their 4-year-old when he screams and cries, the screaming and crying might immediately _____ _____.

In examples, 1, 2, 4, and 5, the behavior will definitely get worse before it gets better. Specifically, in the first example, the toddler will scream louder and longer and may actually say different things (e.g., "I'm coming out now!" or "I don't feel good."). In the second example, the 8-year-old will call his father louder and may say different things (e.g., "I'm calling you!" "I want you here now!"). In the fourth example, the child's asking and complaining might immediately get louder and occur more often. And in the fifth example, the child's screaming and crying will probably get immediately louder and may last longer in the short run.

But what about the third example? In this example, the child has said the bad word only once in front of the parents, and they have only reinforced it once. Although the behavior may get immediately worse (i.e., the child may say the word again and louder), chances are the swearing may not get too much worse and may actually decrease quickly. The reason is that it hasn't been reinforced by the parents' attention before. **A general rule, then, is that the more (or longer) the behavior has been positively reinforced with attention, the more it will burst or increase when that attention is withheld, and the longer it will take to decrease.**

Warning No. 3
In some cases, a child might say things that you think can't be ignored, such as "I hate you," or "You're the worst parent," or "I'm going to kill myself." There are two things to note here. First, when the child is really young, he does not know what he is saying. And second, if you feel that you need to respond, count to

10 and think again, because if you say "I know you don't hate me," then you will very likely inadvertently positively _____ those behaviors, which means they will be _____ likely to occur under similar circumstances. Then, you will have a slightly more serious problem on your hands. Because the next time the situation arises, your child may say even more dramatic things. In essence, you may teach your child to be very creative and to invent new disturbing things to say (see Appendix I for why you don't need to answer everything your child says).

Remember that no matter what your child says, you must continue to ignore. If you don't, you may inadvertently reinforce the new behaviors.

It is instructive to note that in these examples the children are probably not aware that their behavior is increasing, although with adolescents or adults, it is more likely that they might notice that a social positive reinforcer is being withheld. In such instances, they may ask, "Are you ignoring me?" When this happens, the best advice is to answer them with a minimal amount of attention, or to ignore the question. For example, you can pretend to be preoccupied with some other activity, or say "No" or "No, I am not ignoring you," and let it stop there. Or you can try to distract them with another question or activity that you can positively reinforce.

The key to successful planned ignoring is consistency. (Remember the seven factors that make reinforcement work from Chapter 4?). Once you ignore a behavior, continue to ignore it, or you may reinforce successively worse behaviors (e.g., longer, louder screaming and crying, louder calling, or more, or worse, swear words). If you give in with your attention, you will create a much worse problem that will be much more difficult to solve.

But How Will She Learn?

Before moving on, I need to address one concern that I have often heard from parents. Let's go back to the example of the toddler's use of a bad word. When I have suggested that parents use planned ignoring for such behavior, some parents have asked: "How will she ever learn not to use those words if I don't explain that they are not acceptable?" This question represents a fundamental misunderstanding (that I described in Chapter 1) that some parents have about how to teach children, and how children learn to engage in appropriate behavior and not to engage in inappropriate behavior. Just telling your child how to behave or how not to behave will not work.

One of the biggest mistakes parents (and teachers) make with children is to try to reason with or explain to them why they should or should not behave in a particular way. Parents intuitively assume that the only way to teach their children is to talk to them. There are two problems with this approach. The first problem is that parents usually do this right after their child has misbehaved. The result is that the talking often actually reinforces the very behavior the parents don't want their child to engage in by paying attention to it. That means that the child is _____ likely to engage in the bad behavior in similar circumstances. A second problem is that younger children don't understand what the parents are saying anyway. So, rationally explaining something to them, even though it might make you feel better, is a waste of time.

So, how will your sweet little princess ever learn that it's not okay to say that bad word? Because she won't get any attention for it! One of the main points of this book is that we learn by the outcomes of our behavior. When a toddler says that bad word and gets no attention for it, she will stop saying it, at least in those circumstances. This is not to say that someone else, like a teacher or a grandparent, might not pay attention to the behavior. If they do, the child will only, or mostly, say the word with them (in similar circumstances) and not with you (a process called *discrimination*). But you could inform the teacher or grandparent about your approach and enlist their help in practicing the same planned ignoring.

Withholding Negative Reinforcement
In the previous section, I mentioned one of the two reinforcement mistakes parents frequently make: inadvertently reinforcing a child's undesirable behavior. However, I

concentrated solely on inadvertently using positive reinforcement to teach undesirable behavior.

Parents also inadvertently use negative reinforcement to teach undesirable behavior, so it is important to talk about how to undo that. The principle is the same as it is for positive reinforcement: withhold the reinforcer when the undesirable behavior occurs. But we don't call it planned ignoring because **you're not ignoring the behavior**.

Let's consider a common situation. Parents and teachers often place demands on children to do things. For example, a parent may ask a child to "Pick up your toys." Or a teacher may tell a child to "Finish your math problems." If these requests are made, a child may object by saying, "I don't want to." If the parent or teacher then removes the demand by saying, "Okay, you don't have to do it now," they may inadvertently reinforce the child's behavior of negotiating, arguing, or whining — not by adding anything, like attention — but by letting the kid escape from, or subtracting, the demand. Because the demand is removed or subtracted, it is a _____ reinforcer. And we know the subtraction of the demand is reinforcing because the behavior of negotiating or whining may be _____ likely to occur in similar circumstances.

Remember, you can always ask, "What does my child most want now?" If your answer is to get out of having to do something, then it is likely that getting out of it will reinforce whatever behavior gets them out of having to do it, whether it's whining, crying, throwing a tantrum, negotiating, arguing, hitting, etc.

Therefore, to undo the effects of negative reinforcement, the parent or teacher must do the same thing they do when undoing the effects of positive reinforcement: *withhold* the negative reinforcer. Because the negative reinforcer is subtracting or removing something — the demands in the above examples — then you withhold by NOT allowing the child's negotiating, arguing, whining, complaining, etc. to get them out of the demand. In other words, with as little extra attention as possible, the parent must make the kid comply with the request or demand.

It is important to remember, however, that just as with planned ignoring for positive reinforcement, the behavior may immediately get worse because the child will try even harder to get the reinforcer. If that happens, remember to not pay attention while you're ensuring that your child complies with the request or demand. The good news is this burst tells you that you have indeed withheld the negative reinforcer for the undesirable behavior.

Before moving on, try to answer the questions in the examples below.

1. A father asks his daughter to put her toys away, but she starts to cry. So, he tells her she doesn't have to do it now, but she will have to put them away later. Now every time he asks her to do anything, she immediately cries. In order for the father to withhold the reinforcer of his daughter getting out of the demand to put her toys away, he would have to_____.

2. An infant sitting in her highchair starts to cry, so the parents immediately take her out. Now, every time the infant wants to get out of the highchair, she starts to cry. In order for the parents to withhold her getting out of the highchair, they would have to _____.

3. A mother asks her daughter to finish her homework. But the girl argues that it is not due for two days, so she will do it later. The mother says "Okay" and asks her daughter to promise she will do it later. The girl promises that she will. Now every time the mother asks her daughter to do her homework, or anything else, the girl says no and promises that she will do it later. In order for the mother to withhold the reinforcer of her daughter getting out of having to do her homework, she would have to _____
   _____.

In all three examples, the parents would have to not let their kid get out of the request or demand for crying or arguing, preferably by making sure they comply with it. In the first example, the father would make her put her toys away with as little attention as possible. In the third example, the mother would make her daughter finish her homework with as little attention as possible. In the case of the infant in the highchair, the parents should only take her out when she is not crying.

In the first and third examples, when the child does comply, the parents should also positively reinforce the behavior by saying something like, "Thank you for doing what I asked," or "I really like the way you did what I asked." The parents could also use Grandma's Rule and say, "If you do your homework, you can watch TV."

Using Positive Reinforcement
for a Different Behavior

There is another, more desirable, way that the parents in our examples could have dealt with their children's undesirable behaviors. They could have used positive reinforcement to strengthen a *different* behavior than the undesirable one. Researchers call this *reinforcement of alternative behavior.*

Remember the example of the child and parent in the grocery store? Instead of attending to behaviors such as whining or taking things off the shelves, the parent could be aware of when the child is walking quietly. Walking quietly is an alternative to, and incompatible with, whining and taking things off the shelves (they both can't occur at the same time). The parent should then attend to quiet walking either by simply talking to the child or by using specific praise (e.g., "I really like the way you're walking so quietly!"). The parent could also ask the child to help with the shopping by getting things off the shelf or pushing the cart. The parent then gives the child a lot of attention for those behaviors by saying, "Thank you for helping me put things in the cart," or "You really do a great job of putting things in the cart!"). Engaging in desirable behaviors would make it less likely that the child would engage in undesirable behaviors.

Unfortunately, many parents don't recognize when their children are doing what they want and only acknowledge (and inadvertently reinforce) undesirable behavior. Notice how in the five examples at the beginning of this chapter, the parents could have positively reinforced some alternative or incompatible behavior to prevent the undesirable behavior:

1. Instead of the parents going back into a toddler's room when he is crying, they could wait until the toddler is quiet, and <u>then go back in and attend to and/or praise the child. They can require that the child be quiet for longer periods of time every night before going back into the room. Eventually, the child will fall asleep without the parents going into the room.</u>
2. Instead of the father saying "OK," stopping his dish washing, and going to his daughter when she yells at him to "Come help me now!," <u>he could have waited until his daughter was quiet or until she came into the kitchen and asked in a nicer tone, and then helped her.</u> (He also could have prompted her to ask in a more appropriate tone and then stopped to help her. For example, "Can you please come to where I am when you want me?")
3. Instead of the parents chuckling and immediately explaining to their 3-year-old why swear words are not appropriate, <u>they would have to ignore the bad word and wait until she talked about something else, which they could get her to do by asking her about something else, and then give her their undivided attention.</u>
4. Instead of repeating what the child should do or answering the child, <u>the parent could have arranged with the child to earn points for every chore completed and later trade them for other activities or tangible rewards.</u>
5. Instead of hugging and comforting their 4-year-old when he screams and cries when he doesn't get his way, <u>the parents could look for an instance when he doesn't scream or cry and talk to him or tell him what a big boy he is for not crying.</u>

Reinforcing incompatible desirable behavior AND using planned ignoring for undesirable behavior is a winning combination to increase desirable behavior and to decrease or prevent undesirable behavior.

The Secret to Happiness!

No, it's not a lot of money, although it's nice to have money! The secret to having a good relationship with your kid(s) where everyone is happy is this: From the beginning of your child's life, recognize and be aware of behaviors you want your child to exhibit and positively reinforce them, and try not to reinforce any undesirable behaviors. By noticing and positively reinforcing good behavior, you are in a sense inoculating your child against behaving badly.

Before going on, try this brief quiz.

Quiz 6

1. One of the two mistakes parents frequently make is to inadvertently _____ a child's undesirable behavior.

2. The name for withholding positive social reinforcement is _____ *ignoring.*

3. When you withhold positive social reinforcement, you ignore the _____, not the child.

4. When you withhold a positive social reinforcer, there will almost always be a _____ in the behavior, that is the behavior will get _____ before it gets better.

5. In addition to using ignoring, another way that you can deal with undesirable behaviors is to use positive reinforcement to strengthen some behavior _____ than the undesirable one.

6. The best approach to stopping undesirable behavior reinforced by attention is to _____ the undesirable behavior and to _____*ly* _____ any other or incompatible behavior.

7. The opposite of using social positive reinforcement is

_____ _____.

8. It is NOT advisable to use planned ignoring for behaviors that are already _____ and _____.

9. The best approach if your child says things like "I hate you," or "You're the worst parent," or "I'm going to kill myself" is to _____ the behavior.

10. True or False? Young children learn what not to do by the parents reasoning with them. _____

Quiz 6 Answers

1. One of the two mistakes parents frequently make is to inadvertently *reinforce* a child's undesirable behavior.

2. The name for withholding positive social reinforcement is *planned ignoring*.

3. When you withhold positive social reinforcement, you ignore the *behavior*, not the child.

4. When you withhold a positive social reinforcer, there will almost always be a *burst* in the behavior, that is the behavior will get *worse* before it gets better.

5. In addition to using ignoring, another way that you can deal with undesirable behaviors is to use positive reinforcement to strengthen some behavior *other* than the undesirable one.

6. The best approach to stopping undesirable behavior reinforced by attention is to *ignore* the undesirable behavior and to *positively reinforce* any other or incompatible behavior.

7. The opposite of using social positive reinforcement is *planned ignoring*.

8. It is NOT advisable to use planned ignoring for behaviors that are already *dangerous* and *destructive*.

9. The best approach if your child says things like "I hate you," or "You're the worst parent," or "I'm going to kill myself" is to *ignore* the behavior.

10. True or False? Young children learn what not to do by the parents reasoning with them. *False*

Chapter 7: What Is Punishment and How to Use It Effectively and Ethically

A Few Words About Punishment

Many parents often use what they think of as punishment. They reprimand, spank, take privileges away, and send kids to their rooms. But, just as with reinforcement, punishment is only punishment if it produces certain results. Most of the time, however, parents never look to see whether the so-called punishment actually changes behavior in similar circumstances. Even though behavioral scientists usually do not advocate the use of punishment, in some instances it may be necessary or preferred. So, parents need to know how to use and, more importantly, how NOT to use punishment.

What Is Punishment?

As with reinforcement, ***punishment*** is the name given to one of the scientific laws discovered by psychologists. Remember that these are called *laws* because they apply universally. So, what exactly is punishment?

A punisher is defined exactly the same way that a reinforcer is except one word is changed. **A *punisher* is an outcome of a behavior that makes that behavior LESS likely to happen again in similar circumstances.** Just as *to reinforce* means *to strengthen behavior, to punish* means *to weaken behavior*. Reinforcement increases behavior, and punishment decreases behavior. Using punishment is like saying "Don't do it again." For example, if your child draws with crayons on the wall and you immediately take her crayons away for the rest of the day, it's like saying "Don't draw on the wall again." Of course, taking the crayons away is only punishment *if* the child doesn't draw on the wall again.

Punishing the Behavior, Not the Child

Just as we reinforce behavior and not the child, *we also punish behavior and not the child.* The distinction reflects one important difference between how scientific psychologists use the term punishment and how everyone else does. In our culture, we talk about punishing people. This way of talking is understandable because it is derived from a standard definition of punishment as inflicting a penalty on someone as retribution for an offense. But punishment as a universal psychological law is different. *Punishment refers to an outcome of behavior that results in that behavior decreasing under similar circumstances* — and that is all. That is why we say that we *punish a behavior* because we want to decrease the behavior. We are not interested in retribution or revenge; we are only interested in decreasing a specific behavior. This approach results in treating people more ethically.

Types of Punishment

Just as there are two kinds of reinforcement, there are two kinds of punishment: positive and negative. As with reinforcement, positive doesn't mean good, and negative doesn't mean bad. *Positive* **simply means that something is given, or added**, as in addition (+); *negative* **means that something is taken away, or subtracted**, as in subtraction (-).

We classify the types of punishment, in part, by whether they are added or subtracted. For example, because a spanking is added after behavior, it's positive (remember we call a consequence positive only if it is _____, not whether it feels or looks good or bad). In the example above of the child drawing on the wall, because the parents subtracted or took away the crayons, it is an example of _____ punishment.

But rather than giving you examples of positive and negative punishment, let's look at some of the most common types of what people refer to as punishment in terms of their advantages and disadvantages. We begin with the most controversial type of punishment — physical punishment — in particular, spanking.

Physical Punishment

You need to know that most psychologists do not support the use of spanking, hitting, screaming, or any other type of physical force. However, if you're going to use any of these tactics, you need to understand some rules.

First, only use them for behaviors that involve potential harm to the child or others, such as running into the street or playing with a knife. It is not a good idea to use spanking for screaming, throwing tantrums, or crying because the child is already crying, and spanking may make him cry more. There are more appropriate punishment techniques (see below).

Second, if you're going to spank or reprimand, do it immediately and do it forcefully. The spanking must be severe without causing harm to the child. This is because you don't want to have to spank more than a couple of times. If you start out with a gentle paddling, it may not work as punishment (i.e., it may not decrease the undesirable behavior under similar circumstances), and then you will have to gradually increase the force of the spanking. Over time, you may end up hitting your child very hard with no effect because you have taught the child to endure gradually harder and harder spankings.

Psychologists oppose the use of spanking, hitting, or screaming for several reasons. Here are three of the most important: First, using any kind of physical force models it under certain circumstances and shows your child how to use physical force on others (e.g., dolls, pets, friends, and, ultimately, their own children) (see Appendix I). Second, it makes children not like the person who spanks or screams at them, and they are likely to feel fearful and anxious around that person. Third, the child may try to escape and avoid the person who uses the physical force.

Another problem with physical force is that it often doesn't work as punishment, meaning it doesn't decrease the behavior it immediately follows. Thus, parents who continue to spank their children are not punishing behavior but abusing the child and, ironically, possibly reinforcing the very behaviors they are punishing the child for. After all, the spanking is added; and if the child continues to behavior in inappropriate ways, the spanking may be a positive reinforcer. All these problems would not concern us as much if there weren't some better alternatives.

Ironically, the better alternative to physical force and most types of positive punishment is negative punishment. It is ironic because most people equate negative with bad. But, as I've already discussed, negative only means that a consequence is _____ after a behavior.

Types of Negative Punishment

Response Cost

As the name implies, in this negative punishment technique, a child's response *costs* her something. Just as speeding sometimes costs you money (though not consistently), a child's response of drawing on the walls costs her the crayons. Because response cost involves taking something away from the child after some undesirable behavior, it is a form of *negative punishment*, negative because something is _____, and it is punishment *only* if the behavior is _____ likely to occur under similar circumstances.

When using response cost, it is recommended to use what some practitioners refer to as *logical consequences*. In other words, the consequence (the subtraction of something) is logically related to the misbehavior. In the example of the child drawing with crayons on the wall, it is logical to take the crayons away, although conceivably anything could be taken away and still work as a punisher. In the examples below, say what logical consequence the parent could remove using response cost.

- If your child rides his bicycle over your newly planted flower bed, you can remove the _____. The response of _____ costs the child his _____.

- If your child throws her dolls at her baby brother, you can remove the _____. The response of _____ costs the child her _____.
- If your son plays video games instead of doing his homework, you can remove the _____. The response of _____ costs the child his _____.

It is important to note that when using response cost, you should remove the objects for a reasonable amount of time; long enough to work as punishment, but not too long to be unenforceable. For example, if you take TV privileges away from a child, it would not be reasonable or easy to enforce the removal of TV privileges for 2 months. You may have to experiment with different lengths of time to find the optimal one for your child.

Time-Out (From Positive Reinforcement)

Time-out from positive reinforcement — or time-out — is one of the most often misused and abused forms of negative punishment. Because it is a preferred alternative to physical force for certain behaviors, it is important that you know how to use it correctly.

Time-out from positive reinforcement is exactly what the name describes. It is a period during which the child is removed from sources of social positive reinforcement. For example, suppose a 7-year-old begins to throw a tantrum when he doesn't get his way. As you have already learned, tantrums only occur because they are reinforced, either by (1) parents or teachers giving in and giving kids what they want, (2) attending to the tantrums, for example, by talking to the kids and trying to "calm them down," or explaining why they can't get what they want (all positive reinforcers), or (3) letting the kid out of a demand or request to do something (negative reinforcement) (see Appendix I). With time-out, the child would be immediately removed from the situation and placed in a boring place for a pre-specified period of time until the behavior has stopped. If the behavior decreases in the future under similar circumstances, the time-out has functioned as a punisher, specifically a negative punisher, *negative* because something has been _____, and a *punisher* because the behavior that immediately preceded it is _____ likely to occur under similar circumstances.

In addition to being a negative punishment procedure, the time-out period itself involves *planned ignoring*. When time-out begins, the behavior that earned a time-out will often increase immediately and sometimes dramatically. This is the burst I mentioned in the previous chapter. At this time children may say things to parents such as "I hate you" or "You're a terrible Mom" or "I'm going to kill myself." This is the point when the parent must ignore those behaviors. If the parent attends to those statements by answering the child, it may positively _____ those behaviors, meaning that the next time, they would be _____ likely to occur under similar circumstances.

Some kids will say things like, "I promise I'll be good, Dad. Please let me out," or "I won't misbehave anymore, Mom. Can I come out now?" In these instances, I hope you know that you are not to let them out. They earned the time-out for behaving in a certain way, and you have already explained how it works, so they must remain in time-out for the specified amount of time.

Time-out from positive reinforcement is most effective, and therefore only recommended for, certain behaviors that we may call loss-of-control. Such behaviors include throwing tantrums, screaming, swearing, and talking back, as well as aggressive and destructive behaviors. However, because the behavior will likely increase immediately, parents must be careful when using time-out for injurious or destructive behaviors. Those behaviors will get worse and can potentially cause great harm. In such cases, you need to remember to place the child in a setting where she cannot destroy anything of value or hurt herself, because once in time-out, you CANNOT go in or talk to the child.

However, as I said, time-out is very often misused. Therefore, I list the steps to follow in using time-out in Table 7.1.

==

Table 7.1
Steps to Follow When Using Time-Out [1]

1. Talk to your spouse or significant other and agree on using time-out, and then how and when. The parents/adults must be on the same page.

2. Time-out is only recommended for children from approximately 2 to 12 years of age — 2 because they need to be old enough to understand what you're doing and 12 because after that they are getting too big.

3. You must first define and then measure the undesirable behavior you want to target for at least a week prior to beginning time-out (see Chapter 8).

4. Before you actually use time-out, you must explain the time-out procedure to the child, including what behavior will earn her a time-out, where she will go and for how long (1 minute for every year of age). But DO NOT explain it to her right after she has misbehaved, or you might inadvertently reinforce her misbehavior.

5. When the undesirable behavior occurs, you say only 4 words — "Time-out for _____." For example, "Time-out for screaming." Escort the child to the time-out area with little or no other attention and set a timer. The reason to set a timer is so that you won't forget, and also so that both you and the child can hear when the timer times out (see Appendix I).

6. When the timer goes off, and only if the child is quiet, you may let her out of time-out. If she is still behaving undesirably, you must reset the timer (for another minute or two) and keep doing that until the child is quiet.

7. When time-out is over, there is no need to explain to your child why she went to time out (you already did that before you began using it), or to make her apologize, or to talk to her about her undesirable behavior. You should also respond to her comments about it with minimal reaction. You should resume your normal interactions as if nothing happened and begin to positively reinforce desirable behavior.

---

[1] These are the main steps in using time-out. For a more complete discussion, see Clark, 1996.

===

Because the correct use of time-out is so important, let's look at an example.

- The 3-year-old I mentioned in Chapter 1 would hit his mother when she wouldn't let him have what he wanted. So, once she decided to try time-out, she sat him down at a time when he wasn't angry and explained what she and her husband were going to do. She then asked her son to repeat back to her what would happen and when, so she knew he understood. At the first instance of hitting, she said, "Time-out for hitting," and promptly escorted him to the time-out room, which was the bathroom. She immediately set a timer for 3 minutes (1 minute for every year of age) and placed it outside the bathroom door so they could both hear it when it timed out. He immediately began screaming and yelling "I hate you." Difficult as it was for her to hear this, she was a real trooper and ignored the screaming. When the 3 minutes were up, her son was still screaming, so she added more time — another minute — without saying anything to him because she and her husband had already explained the rules. After adding a few more minutes, the screaming and yelling subsided. So, when the timer timed out next, and her son was quiet, she opened the door to let him out. She said no more about it and resumed her normal interactions with him. Over the next few weeks, she had to use time-out a few more times, but each time, the behavior subsided more quickly. After a few weeks, her son was only very rarely hitting her. Just as importantly, the mother reinforced more acceptable behavior when her son didn't get what he wanted, which competed with the hitting and screaming. As a result, both mother and son were much happier.

  Remember, the behaviors you've identified to use time-out for have been reinforced, albeit inadvertently; that is why they occur in the first place. Remember, also, that the longer the behavior has been reinforced, the longer it will take to decrease when you start using time-out. So, even though your child may not be happy in time-out, ask yourself if she's happy screaming, crying, and throwing tantrums. At least there is light at the end of the tunnel if you use the time-out procedure correctly.

Contingent Observation

A punishment procedure that is related to time-out is called *contingent observation*. This is a technique that can be used with a child who is misbehaving in a group of other children, which can include siblings, friends, or classmates. Consider the following example.

My son had a birthday party, which included a magic show, and one of the boys, we'll call him Charles, was saying inappropriate things and interrupting the magic show with comments like "This is stupid." So, I said, "Charles, go stand in the corner." He looked at me like no one had ever made him do anything like that before. But he complied and stood in the corner and watched — *observed* — the other kids having fun with the magic show. After 60 seconds, I told him he could go sit down. A few minutes later, he said something else inappropriate, and once again I said, "Charles, go stand in the corner." He gave me the same evil eye look but complied. This time I waited 120 seconds, during which he had to watch — *observe* — the other kids having fun. Then I told him to go and sit back down. After that, he behaved like an angel, and I even went over to him and patted him on the head and told him how nicely he was sitting (specific praise).

So, *contingent* on his bad behavior, he was made to leave the group and *observe* them having fun — contingent observation. Then his inappropriate behavior stopped, and he displayed more appropriate behavior that I could praise.

The Premack Principle of Punishment

Remember that I introduced the Premack Principle of reinforcement (aka Grandma's Rule) briefly in Chapter 4, and then in Chapter 5 I talked in more detail about using preferred activities to reinforce less preferred behaviors. The same logic can also be used with punishment. For example, suppose your child constantly throws his toy on the floor. When he has done so in the past, you have told him to pick it up and explained why he shouldn't throw toys. But he hasn't stopped doing it. What can you do?

You could try using response cost in which he loses the toy for a brief specified amount of time immediately after he throws it. Or you could use the Premack Principle of punishment, in which case he would have to engage in some less preferred activity. In this example, a less preferred activity that is logically related to throwing toys would be for him to pick up the toy he threw.

You can sometimes use the Premack Principle of punishment even more effectively by making the child engage in even more of the less preferred activity. So, in the example above, when the child throws a toy, not only does he have to pick up that toy, but he has to pick up everything on the floor (aka *overcorrection*). It's kind of like making the child work very hard after an undesirable behavior.

One problem with using this strategy is that the child might refuse to pick up the toys. Then you would be in a position of having to force him to do so, and that might turn into a struggle. In such cases, you should physically, but gently, guide him to pick up the toys and praise him for doing it while ignoring any complaining or crying, etc.

The Ethical Use of Punishment

I am not promoting the use of punishment. On the other hand, sometimes it is necessary to decrease some behavior. Moreover, like reinforcement, punishment is a part of our natural environment. For example, if you are careless and accidentally slam the car door on your finger, you will be less likely to do that again. Having your finger slammed in the door will punish the careless behavior in that it will be _____ likely to occur again under similar circumstances. There are numerous examples of naturally occurring punishment.

Based on the discussion in this chapter, if you do want to use punishment, you should opt for one of the negative punishment strategies. Remember, they are called negative because something is _____, or removed, right after an undesirable behavior. And they are only called punishment if the behavior is _____ likely to occur under similar circumstances.

Also remember, if you want to punish a behavior, it means that it has probably already been reinforced. For example, suppose your child argues with you, and you argue back. At first you hardly notice her arguing behavior. But after a while, you realize that it occurs often and lasts a long time. It has become a big problem. You want to decrease the arguing, so you decide to use some type of punishment. While this plan sounds reasonable, it is very unfair to your child. Why? Because you're the one who taught her to argue in the first place by inadvertently reinforcing it.

The same problem would occur for a child who throws a tantrum when he doesn't get his way, but the parent frequently gives in. If the parent now decides to punish the tantrums, it is unfair to the child.

Your best bet is to positively reinforce good behaviors when they occur. If you do this, there won't be many times when you will even think about using punishment (see Chapter 13). But if you do decide to punish a behavior, it should be a last resort.

Before going on, try this brief quiz.

Quiz 7

1. Punishment is called a *law* because it applies _____.

2. A *punisher* is any usually immediate _____ of a behavior that makes the behavior _____ likely to happen again.

3. *Positive* simply means that the punisher is _____, as in addition (+); and *negative* means that the punisher is _____, as in subtraction (-).

4. Hitting (spanking) and screaming are types of _____ punishers.

5. One problem with using such punishers is that the parents are _____ physical force under certain circumstances and showing their child how to use such force on others.

6. The punishment technique in which some potential positive reinforcer, such as a toy or a privilege, is taken away when a child misbehaves is called _____ cost.

7. If the consequence that is taken away is related to the undesirable behavior, it is said to be a _____ consequence.

8. When the child is removed from a positively reinforcing situation contingent on some undesirable behavior, the punishment technique is called _____-_____ from positive reinforcement.

9. When using this technique in #8 for hitting, for example, you should only say four words to your child: _____-_____ for _____.

10. Because the techniques in #6-8 involve removing something after an undesirable behavior, they are examples of _____ punishers.

Quiz 7 Answers

1. Punishment is called a *law* because it applies *universally*.

2. A *punisher* is any usually immediate *outcome (or consequence)* of a behavior that makes the behavior *less* likely to happen again.

3. There are two kinds of punishment: positive and negative. *Positive* simply means that the punisher is *added*, as in addition (+); and *negative* means that the punisher is *subtracted (or removed or taken away)*, as in subtraction (-).

4. Hitting (spanking) and screaming are types of *physical* punishers.

5. One problem with using such punishers is that the parents are *modeling* physical force under certain circumstances and showing their child how to use such force on others.

6. The punishment technique in which some potential positive reinforcer, such as a toy or a privilege, is taken away when a child misbehaves is called *response* cost.

7. If the consequence that is taken away is related to the undesirable behavior, it is said to be a *logical* consequence.

8. When the child is removed from a positively reinforcing situation contingent on some undesirable behavior, the punishment technique is called *time-out* from positive reinforcement.

9. When using this technique in #8 for hitting, for example, you should only say four words to your child: *time-out* for *hitting*.

10. Because the techniques in #6-8 involve removing something after an undesirable behavior, they are examples of *negative* punishers.

Part IV – How to Build Good Behavior and Self Esteem Using Positive Reinforcement

Chapter 8: Five Steps to Changing Behavior

The five steps to changing behavior are:

1. Identify the behavior to be changed.

2. Select the positive reinforcer.

3. Measure the behavior.

4. Apply (or withhold) the positive reinforcer.

5. Evaluate the behavior change.

Now you know what positive reinforcement is, how to use it, and how not to use it. You also know how to undo the effects of the positive (or negative) reinforcement of undesirable behavior through planned ignoring and punishment and the use of positive reinforcement of alternative or incompatible behavior. You are now ready to think about a program for changing behavior in your child.

As the title of this chapter indicates, there are five steps to follow in any behavior change program using positive reinforcement (and/or planned ignoring).

Step 1: Identifying the Behavior to Change

The first step in changing behavior using positive reinforcement (and/or planned ignoring) is to identify the behavior you want to change *and* the circumstances under which it occurs or under which you would like it to occur.

Although this step sounds simple, it is actually one of the more difficult things for most people. For example, suppose a father tells you that his son is "strong-willed." You might know intuitively what he means, but if you asked 10 different people what that means, you'd get 10 different descriptions. So, you need to ask this father exactly what he means. Suppose he says, "You know, my son has a mind of his own." Is that any better? Do you know any more than before? No. So, you ask the father, "What does your son do?" And he replies, "He always has to get his way." Is this an improvement? Obviously not much. I hope you see the difficulty this father has in simply telling you what behaviors his son engages in that lead him to call his son "strong-willed." So, you try again by saying, "But tell me, what does he do and when does he do it? Does he cry, scream, or hit when he asks for something and you don't let him have it?" Now the father understands what you're asking and replies, "Oh, I see what you mean. Yeah, when we won't let him have what he wants, he cries and screams." Now you know what behaviors to target — screaming and crying — and under what circumstances they occur — when he doesn't get what he wants.

Because these behaviors are ones you want to decrease, let's try another example involving behavior(s) you would want to increase. Suppose a parent tells you that her daughter is lazy and unmotivated. Again, what does this mean? So, you ask the mother "Exactly _____?" (You're right if you said, "Exactly what does your daughter do and when?") Suppose the parent says that her daughter doesn't do her schoolwork, doesn't study, and is on her phone instead. Now we know what she means by lazy.

In an example like this one, however, we might discover that the girl is only "lazy" and "unmotivated" in some settings, such as school or when she has to do schoolwork but not in other settings, such as when she is playing video games or on her phone. Such information tells us that there is something about the schoolwork that is contributing to her "laziness" and "lack of motivation."

The problem with using terms like "strong-willed" or "a mind of his own," or even "aggressive," "hurtful," "selfish," "shy," "nasty," "lazy," "unmotivated," or "depressed" is that these terms are, at best, only labels for a variety of behaviors. They don't tell you exactly what the child is doing and when. You can't change lazy or unmotivated or strong-willed, but you can change doing homework, crying, or screaming. As an exercise, try to list three behaviors that one might observe in a child for some of these labels.

- aggressive - _____, _____, _____
- hurtful - _____, _____, _____
- selfish - _____, _____, _____
- shy - _____, _____, _____
- lazy - _____, _____, _____
- depressed - _____, _____, _____

Let's see some behaviors that fit these labels.
- aggressive - <u>hits, bites, kicks</u>
- hurtful - <u>says "You're ugly," criticizes, makes fun of others</u>
- selfish - <u>won't share toys with others, won't offer food to others, won't let others play with his video games</u>
- shy - <u>doesn't make eye contact, looks down, speaks too quietly to be heard</u>
- lazy - <u>doesn't finish homework, doesn't do chores, doesn't put clothes away</u>
- depressed - <u>rarely smiles, complains a lot, cries often</u>

As you can see, these and many other labels we use to describe behavior are somewhat vague and unhelpful when we want to target specific behaviors to change. Also, the specific descriptions of the behaviors don't tell the whole story. In other words, they don't tell you when the behaviors occur. And the *when*, that is, under what circumstances, is just as important in being able to figure out *why* the behaviors occur. For example, it's not enough to know that a child cries when asked to do something. If he cries when the father asks him but not when the mother asks him, that is a clue which suggests that the father is reinforcing crying and the mother is not.

Step 2: Selecting the Positive Reinforcer

Once you've selected a behavior, the second step in using positive reinforcement is to select the particular positive reinforcer you want to use.

As discussed in Chapter 5, there are many different types of reinforcers you can use. Selecting the best reinforcer depends on several factors. But perhaps the most important factor is what you think will work the best at a particular time. As I indicated previously, using Grandma's Rule is always a safe bet. In that case, all you have to do is figure out what the child wants to do at a particular moment, usually by watching what she does or having her tell you what she wants to do, and then restrict that activity until she does what you want her to do. Of course, no matter what other reinforcers you use, you can always use praise and social attention when the desirable behavior occurs.

Step 3: Measuring the Behavior

The third step in using positive reinforcement is to count (or measure) the behavior. Why should you count the behavior? The answer is simple: so that you can know with some accuracy whether your skillful use of positive reinforcement has indeed increased the desirable behavior, or whether, in your unbridled optimism about your success, you just think it has. Remember, our perceptions and memories are usually not very accurate representations of what has really happened. So, count the behavior.

There is more than one way to count a behavior. First, you can count the number of times a behavior occurs in a certain period of time (called *frequency*), such as the number of times a child calls out someone's name, the number of times a child hits, or the number of times a child says please when she asks for something. Second, you can count the amount of time a person spends doing something (called *duration*), for example, how long a child spends playing, talking on the phone, throwing a tantrum, etc. For some behaviors, it may be helpful to count both. Third, you can measure the latency of the behavior you want to occur. For example, suppose you ask your 4-year-old to pick up his crayons from the floor. You can then count how many seconds, or minutes, it takes him to comply.

Once you have decided *what* behavior to count and *how* to count it, you need to put your count down on paper. This is usually a two-step process. First, you simply write the number (whether it is frequency, duration, or latency) on a tally sheet (as shown below). Second, you transfer the data from the tally sheet to a graph. The importance of graphing your behavior count is that a graphic representation will help you to see exactly at what level the behavior is occurring and whether there are any patterns or trends.

It is always a good idea to begin counting the behavior BEFORE you apply the positive reinforcer. In research terms, this period of counting the behavior before you try to positively reinforce it is called *baseline*. The baseline is just that, a basis for evaluating whether your positive reinforcer really worked, that is whether it actually _____ the behavior you selected. Remember that during baseline, you simply count or measure the behavior WITHOUT trying to change it. That means that you do whatever you normally do when the behavior occurs.

Date	Count	Total	Comments

Step 4: Applying (or Withholding) the Positive Reinforcer

The fourth step is to actually apply (or withhold) the positive reinforcer. In order to do this successfully, you need to remember the seven things that make positive reinforcement work.

So, let's try a little review quiz. For positive reinforcement to be most effective:

1. The reinforcer must _____ the child.
2. The child must _____ the positive reinforcer.
3. A positive reinforcer must be added _____
after the desired behavior.
4. The positive reinforcer must occur only _____ the
behavior you want to increase.
5. The positive reinforcer must be relatively _____ in
size.
6. If you want the behavior to persist, you must reinforce it

_____.
7. A positive reinforcer must occur _____ after a
desired behavior.

How did you do? If you answered *want, immediately* or *very soon, after, large, intermittently,* and *consistently,* then you did well!

Based on these seven considerations, you must wait for the behavior to occur and then immediately allow the child to engage in her preferred activity and/or add your attention or praise. And remember, to give your attention or allow access to a preferred activity ONLY for the behavior you want to increase (contingency).

Step 5: Evaluating the Behavior Change

The fifth step is to evaluate whether the use of positive reinforcement has really increased the targeted behavior. Is the outcome you selected really a reinforcer? In order to know this, you must graph your totals. (Graphs and data sheets are available for download on the book's website).

Let's briefly review these five steps.

Step 1: Identifying the Behavior to Be Changed
The behavior must be identified in terms that can be observed and measured. So, *aggression* is not a good term; *hitting* is. *Shyness* is not a good term; *speaking softly and not making eye contact* are. *Cleaning your room* isn't a precise description; *picking up your toys and putting them in the closet* is.

Step 2: Identifying the Positive Reinforcer to Be Used
You must have an idea that the positive reinforcer will work for the child, and the child must want it. Is it going to be attention, a tangible object, an activity or privilege, or points on a chart?

Step 3: Measuring (and Graphing) the Behavior
You can count the number of times the behavior occurs (frequency) or the amount of time the behavior lasts (duration), or how quickly the behavior occurs (latency). And you need to measure and graph the behavior several days BEFORE you apply the positive reinforcer (baseline).

Step 4: Applying (or Withholding) the Positive Reinforcer
You must add the reinforcer immediately after the behavior keeping in mind the six factors that make reinforcement more effective.

Step 5: Evaluating the Behavior Change
This is accomplished by simply looking at your graph of the behavior both before and after the reinforcer was added.

Before going on, try this brief quiz.

Quiz 8

1. The first step in using positive reinforcement to increase a desirable behavior is to _____ the behavior you want to increase.

2. But you not only need to know what the behavior is, you need to know the _____ under which it occurs.

3. The second step in using positive reinforcement is to _____ the particular positive reinforcer you want to use.

4. The third step in using positive reinforcement is to _____ (or _____) the behavior.

5. If you measure the *number* of times a behavior occurs in a certain period of time, this is called _____.

6. If you measure the *amount* of time a behavior occurs, this is called _____.

7. The period of measuring a behavior before you try to positively reinforce it is called _____.

8. During this period, you simply measure the behavior without trying to _____ it.

9. The fourth step in using positive reinforcement is to actually apply the _____ _____.

10. The fifth, and final, step in using positive reinforcement is to evaluate whether the use of positive reinforcement has really _____ the targeted behavior.

Quiz 8 Answers

1. The first step in using positive reinforcement to increase a desirable behavior is to *identify* the behavior you want to increase.

2. But you not only need to know what the behavior is, you need to know the *circumstances* under which it occurs.

3. The second step in using positive reinforcement is to *select* the particular positive reinforcer you want to use.

4. The third step in using positive reinforcement is to *count* (or *measure*) the behavior.

5. If you measure the *number* of times a behavior occurs in a certain period of time, this is called *frequency*.

6. If you measure the *amount* of time a behavior occurs, this is called *duration*.

7. The period of measuring a behavior before you try to positively reinforce it is called *baseline*.

8. During this period, you simply measure the behavior without trying to *change* it.

9. The fourth step in using positive reinforcement is to actually apply the *positive reinforcer*.

10. The fifth, and final, step in using positive reinforcement is to evaluate whether the use of positive reinforcement has really *increased* the targeted behavior.

Chapter 9: Two Examples of Using Positive Reinforcement

Before you carry out your own exercise, let's take a look at two examples: a hypothetical example and then a real example.

Example 1: A Hypothetical Example
The following represents a hypothetical example of how a parent might get her daughter to spend more time reading.

Step 1: Identifying the Behavior to Be Changed
A mother wants to increase the amount of time her 5-year-old daughter spends reading.

Step 2: Identifying the Positive Reinforcer to Be Used
The social positive reinforcer she decides to use is a combination of specific praise, such as "Kathy, I'm really proud of you for reading," and general interaction/talking, such as "What are you reading?" and "What is it about?"

Step 3: Measuring the Behavior
The data sheet below indicates how long (in minutes) Kathy read each day (duration) over 14 days, both when she was told to by her mother and when she read without being asked.

Date	Behavior	Total	Comments
1/01	10'	10'	Read when told to
1/02	7'	7'	Read when told to
1/03	8'	8'	Initiated reading.
1/04	13'	13'	Initiated reading.
1/05	12'	12'	Read when told to
1/06	10'	10'	Read when told to
1/07	12'	12'	Initiated reading
1/08	15'	15'	Initiated
1/09	16'	16'	Initiated
1/10	20'	20'	Initiated
1/11	17'	17'	Initiated
1/12	20'	20'	Initiated
1/13	18'	18'	Initiated
1/14	20'	20'	Initiated

Days 1 through 5 were the baseline. Beginning on day 6, the mother began to praise Kathy for reading and continued to count the behavior.

Steps 4 and 5: Applying the Positive Reinforcer and Evaluating the Behavior Change
    To evaluate whether the exercise was successful, the mother plotted the data from the tally sheet.

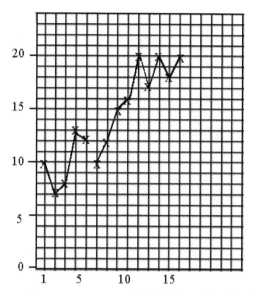

As you can see, during baseline Kathy did not read for more than 13 minutes on a single day, and the average (10 + 8 + 7 + 13 + 12 = 50/5 [days]) was 10 minutes per day. Therefore, the mother decided that a reasonable goal would be to try to increase reading to more than 10 minutes per day. Also, if you look at the comments in the tally sheet, you can see that the mother had to tell Kathy to read during baseline, but Kathy initiated reading on her own exclusively after the mother began using positive reinforcement.

After the mother started using social positive reinforcement for reading, you can see that Kathy began spending more time reading (up to an average of 16.5 minutes per day), indicating that the social praise and interaction was probably a reinforcer for the behavior.

Example 2: A Real Example

The following example is based on two projects carried out by students in one of my developmental psychology classes. Although the projects involved two different children (a 2-year-old girl and a 3-year-old girl), they both dealt with a similar problem. In both cases, the girls screamed when they wanted something, and although both knew some words, they rarely used them to communicate. In fact, the family of the 3-year-old feared that she might have a developmental problem such as autism because she wasn't talking at an age-appropriate level. The following example represents a synthesis of these two experiments with data from one of them.

Step 1: Identifying the Behavior to Be Changed

The goal was to increase the number of words and to decrease the number of screams that the little girls used to communicate with others. Often when kids scream or cry, they could actually talk and tell you what they want. So, you will want to increase their talking under the same circumstances in which they would normally cry or scream. Of course, just because they might tell you what they want instead of cry or scream doesn't mean you should necessarily give in to them. After all, we don't always get what we want just by telling someone.

Step 2: Identifying the Positive Reinforcer to Be Used

For these two little girls, screaming was positively reinforced when others gave them what they wanted. (Of course, family members' and teachers' behaviors of giving in were negatively reinforced because the screaming stopped — see Appendix I.) The key was to make the social positive reinforcers of answering the little girls and giving them what they want *dependent* on some behavior *other* than screaming (an alternative and incompatible behavior: using words) and to use *planned ignoring* for the screaming.

Step 3: Measuring the Behavior

Before using positive reinforcement to change the behaviors, we needed to know how often both the appropriate and inappropriate behaviors were occurring. The number of screams and of appropriate words were counted on days 1-10 during *baseline*. The graph below shows the baseline for the 2-year-old.

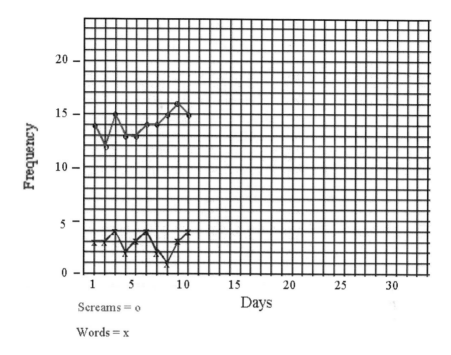

Screams = o

Words = x

Step 4: Applying the Positive Reinforcer

We already identified the positive reinforcer as social attention for using appropriate words and giving them what they want and withholding the same for screams. More specifically, when the little girls screamed, the screams were ignored; and when they used words, the adults used specific praise and gave them what they wanted. Also, with the 2-year-old, the adult would hold up an object that the little girl wanted and have her repeat the name (called a *prompt*) whereupon she would immediately get the object (a tangible positive reinforcer).

Step 5: Evaluating the Program

Now let's see what effect these procedures had both on screaming and using words. First, based on what we said in Chapter 6 about the effects of withholding a positive reinforcer from a well-reinforced behavior, you would predict that the behavior of screaming should _____ immediately when attention for screaming is withheld (Remember that we called that a *burst?*). (If you said increase, you'd be correct.) Look at the graph below on days 11-16, and you'll notice that not only did the number of screams increase, but the number of words decreased. It would be very tempting at this point for someone not in the know to conclude that the program was not working and to discontinue it. However, you know that the best plan of action is to be consistent, because the increase in screaming — the burst — was predicted BEFORE the program started.

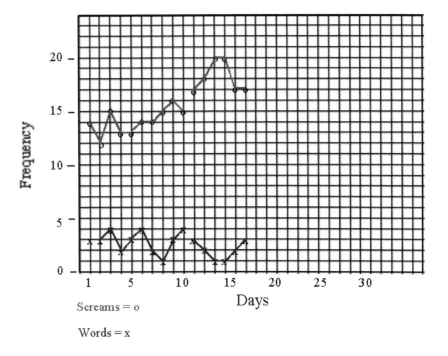

If you look at days 16-30 on the graph below, you'll see that the number of screams decreased and the number of appropriate words increased dramatically. They actually switched places on the graph. This indicates that both positive reinforcement for using words and planned ignoring for screaming had their intended effect.

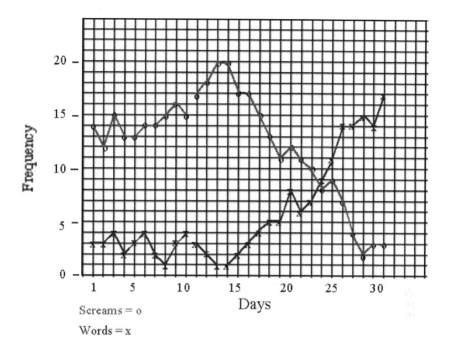

Screams = o
Words = x

Days

In addition to successfully getting the children to use words instead of screaming, we might want to speculate on the difference this makes for the children (and others in their lives). For example, the 2-year-old had bad asthma, and screaming would exacerbate her asthma, so learning to speak instead of scream had significant health benefits. Less screaming meant fewer asthma attacks. For the 3-year-old, it became apparent that her language problem wasn't developmental in origin but environmental. As a result of her language improving, she didn't need to be sent to a child psychologist or a pediatrician for diagnosis and treatment. Plus, once the kids talked more and screamed less, they were seen as being more pleasant to be around. All involved were happier.

An interesting side note

The project with the 3-year-old was undertaken by her aunt, who watched the little girl during the day when the mother worked. So, during the day, the little girl used a lot of words and screamed very little. As soon as her mother picked her up, the little girl immediately began screaming and using fewer words. This shows even more powerfully the important role of the environment in many problem behaviors. It also shows the same child can behave differently depending on the circumstances.

In fact, this example demonstrates another law of psychology mentioned earlier, called *discrimination*. In this case, the little girl responded differently depending on whether her mother or her aunt was present. How does that happen? Based on what you've learned so far, you might guess that when the little girl screamed in the presence of her mother, the mother _____ the screaming by either paying attention to it or, more importantly, giving the little girl what she wanted. When she talked, the mother may have given her what she wanted or not. When the little girl used her words with the aunt, the aunt immediately gave her what she asked for (within reason); and when she screamed, the aunt _____ the screaming and did not give her what she wanted.

As a result of having her talking and screaming responded to differently by the mother and the aunt, the little girl's behavior conformed to each adult. Because the little girl was 3, she didn't understand what she was doing or why. This brings up another important point: **A child does not have to understand what the parents are doing in order for her behavior to change**.

Before going on, try this brief quiz.

Quiz 9

1. Measuring behavior before you decide to change it with positive reinforcement is called _____ because it gives you a starting point to compare the behavior both before and after you carry out your change procedure.

2. To evaluate whether the change program was successful, you need to _____ the data on a graph.

3. In the real example in this chapter, the behavior to be changed in the two little girls was increasing the number of _____ and decreasing the number of _____.

4. The reinforcers that were used were simply _____ them or _____ them what they wanted when the little girls used words instead of screaming.

5. At the same time, the adults had to _____ the screams.

6. With the 2-year-old, the adult sometimes had her repeat the name of what she wanted, called a _____.

7. The improvement in the 2-year-old's behavior had an unintended consequence, namely that not screaming had health benefits. Screaming caused her to have _____.

8. After the change program, the 3-year-old talked more and screamed less with the aunt, who carried out the program, but still screamed with the mother. This illustrates another law of behavior called _____.

9. The result in #8 occurred because the aunt _____ly _____ed talking, not screaming, whereas the mother still _____ed screaming.

10. It is important to remember that a child does not have to _____ or be aware of what the parents are doing in order for her behavior to change.

Quiz 9 Answers

1. Measuring behavior before you decide to change it with positive reinforcement is called *baseline* because it gives you a starting point to compare the behavior both before and after you carry out your change procedure.

2. To evaluate whether the change program was successful, you need to *plot* the data on a graph.

3. In the real example in this chapter, the behavior to be changed in the two little girls was increasing the number of *words they used* and decreasing the number of *screams*.

4. The reinforcers that were used were simply *answering (or talking to)* them or *giving* them what they wanted when the little girls used words instead of screaming.

5. At the same time, the adults had to *ignore* the screams.

6. With the 2-year-old, the adult sometimes had her repeat the name of what she wanted, called a *prompt*.

7. The improvement in the 2-year-old's behavior had an unintended consequence, namely that not screaming had health benefits. Screaming caused her to have *asthma*.

8. After the change program, the 3-year-old talked more and screamed less with the aunt, who carried out the program, but still screamed with the mother, which illustrates another law of behavior called *discrimination*.

9. The result in #8 occurred because the aunt *positively reinforced* talking, not screaming, whereas the mother still *reinforced* screaming.

10. It is important to remember that a child does not have to *understand* or be aware of what the parents are doing in order for her behavior to change.

Chapter 10: Five Brief Case Studies

Now you have seen how social positive reinforcement and planned ignoring could be used in a theoretical example and were used to change the behavior of two preschool children in a real example. To give you a better idea of types of behaviors that can be changed with positive reinforcement, in this chapter I describe five other examples of how positive (social) reinforcement was used to improve the behaviors of children of different ages.

Case 1: Can You Please Speak Up?

In this case, a 7-year-old girl spoke so quietly that people around her were always asking, "Sorry, honey, what did you say?" or "Could you please speak up?" Sometimes family members would sit her down and talk to her about her quiet speaking, saying, "If you can't make yourself heard, people will ignore you." Often, we just label such behavior "shyness" and assume kids are born with it, which not only doesn't explain the behavior, but also doesn't remedy it either. Worse, the adults' attention in the form of asking her to repeat herself was probably acting as a _____ _____er for the very behaviors they didn't want.

In this case, the adults began a program of planned ignoring for quiet speaking under the assumption that it was their attention that positively reinforced the quiet speaking in the first place. The adults also listened for instances of louder talking and responded to those by giving the girl what she wanted or just talking to her (reinforcing alternative and incompatible behaviors — you can't talk quietly and loudly at the same time). During baseline, the number of times she spoke too quietly to be heard averaged 13.35 per day. By the last five days of the project, it had decreased to zero, which meant that she was talking loudly enough to be heard. An added advantage was that the little girl also felt better about herself and seemed more confident. In other words, her self-esteem had also increased. Can you guess why?

Case 2: Go to Sleep

When put in his crib for a nap, a preschool boy would cry, scream, kick the crib, hit the wall, and stand up. When he did this, his teachers would immediately go over to him and try to calm him down. These reactions by the teachers obviously were functioning as _____ _____*ment* for the little boy's disruptive behaviors because the same behaviors happened every day in the same situation. It is also possible the boy's behaviors were being negatively reinforced. In other words, crying and screaming allowed him to get out of the crib and naptime.

A program of planned ignoring for the disruptive behaviors and social positive reinforcement for lying down and being quiet for a few seconds (in the beginning) was instated. The teacher sat in a chair near the crib, and when the boy was not making any attempts to get out, she would go over to the crib (which she only did before when he was being disruptive) and quietly talk to him and stroke him. If he began to cry or stand up, the teacher would immediately go back to her chair. During baseline, the boy made an average of 10 attempts to get out of the crib during naptime. Needless to say, he wasn't sleeping. After 30 days, he was making zero attempts to get out and was napping.

The benefits were many. First, the child was napping. Second, he learned that he couldn't get the teachers' attention by screaming and crying. Third, he wasn't disrupting the other kids' naptime. And fourth, he was probably happier, and his teachers were too.

Case 3: Please Pick Up Your Things

In three different cases, a 3-year-old, a 6-year-old, and a 9-year-old did not pick up their clothes and toys. In all three cases, the adults wanted their children to comply with a request to "Please pick up your things" and, ultimately, to pick up their things on their own without being asked.

In the case of the 3-year-old, not only did she not pick up her toys when asked, but she would say, "No, I don't want to."

Like most well-intentioned parents, her mother would explain why she had to pick up her toys and why it wasn't nice to talk like that. Of course, this explaining positively reinforced the oppositional behavior of saying "No."

For the 3-year-old, it was decided that social positive reinforcement in the form of hugs and specific praise ("Thank you for picking up your toys" and "I'm so proud of you for picking up your toys") would be used in combination with planned ignoring for talking back.

The 6-year-old girl and her older sister who carried out the project made a chart with the days of the week and space to fill in a "0" when she did not pick up her toys or a "1" when she did pick up her toys. When the little girl got a "1," her sister would use specific praise and say, "Good girl, you're such a big girl for picking up your toys," and occasionally give her a treat.

For the 9-year-old, the father decided to use an activity/privilege reinforcer (staying up 1/2 hour later and watching TV) plus social praise if all items were picked up from the floor by 8 p.m.

Notice how the reinforcers were appropriate for each child's age. Also, because the 9-year-old was old enough, his father could explain to him the new rule (including the behavior expected and the positively reinforcing consequence).

The baseline measurement for all three children was almost zero (and the negative comments by the 3-year-old occurred about 50% of the time). By the end of the projects, each child was complying at almost 100%, and the 3-year-old was no longer making any negative comments. As a result, the rooms were less cluttered, and everyone was happier.

An interesting side note

As the example with the 6-year-old showed, an older sibling can on occasion take the place of a parent. The older sibling can make requests and deliver reinforcement just like a parent would. This has two potential benefits. First, the older sibling learns how to build good behavior using positive reinforcement.

And second, the younger child's behavior changes. It's a win-win-win for everyone.

Case 4: Nobody Likes a Tattle Tale

In this case, the parent was having a problem with an 8-year-old who was "a big tattle tale." The boy would tell the parent each time he thought his older brothers were doing something wrong. When he tattled, his parent would either ask him about it or explain why it is not nice to tattle. By doing this, the parent was unknowingly reinforcing the tattling with attention. During baseline, the frequency of tattling averaged 4.5 times per day, and as you can imagine, it caused a lot of friction in the family.

The parent decided to use a combination of planned ignoring for tattling and social positive reinforcement in the form of specific praise for behaviors other than tattling. As expected, when the planned ignoring for tattling began, the tattling immediately increased (the predicted burst) and reached a peak of 15 times a day, testing the parent's resolve. Eventually, the tattling decreased to fewer than 2 times a day.

An interesting side note

When the tattling disappeared, another disturbing behavior emerged. The 8-year-old began asking if he could tell his siblings how to do things. This is a phenomenon that psychologists call *resurgence*, which means that if one behavior is decreased through planned ignoring, another (sometimes older) behavior might re-emerge. Of course, the parent, now the wiser, immediately ignored this "new" behavior, and it quickly disappeared too.

Case 5: Please Say "Please" or "Thank You"

Most kids eventually learn to say "please" and "thank you," but some don't, and for others it takes longer. Often parents and teachers try to explain why kids should be polite and use manners, but, of course, such reasoning doesn't work most of the time, especially with very young children. In this case, a 4-year-old boy was taught to say "please" and "thank you" at appropriate times. The father counted the number of times the child could have said "please" or "thank you" and the number of times he actually said them. The father used social positive reinforcement in the form of specific praise ("Good job saying 'thank you'"). During baseline, the child said "please" or "thank you" only 14% of the times he could have. The last five days of the project, he was saying "please" or "thank you" 80% of the time.

In such cases with very young children, adults must usually **model** the correct behavior under the appropriate circumstances. That means the parents *show the child the correct way to behave in a particular circumstance*, and then **prompt** the behavior. For example, a parent can say things like, "What do you say?" (which is a prompt) and then model the correct response, "You say 'thank you.'" When the child imitates, the adult uses specific praise such as, "Right. Good job saying 'thank you.'"

Then, the prompts can be gradually removed — called *fading* — while still praising the appropriate behavior. For example, once the child can say "thank you" when the parent says, "What do you say? You say 'thank you,'" the parent can then say "What do you say, you say...." Eventually the parents can simply say "What do you say?" and the child will respond by saying "thank you." Then, if the parent observes the child spontaneously saying "thank you" under appropriate circumstances, they should respond with specific praise, such as "Good job saying 'thank you.'"

I hope that these five cases, plus the other examples provided so far, give you an idea of the range of behaviors for which you can use positive reinforcement. Now you can try to do it on your own. On the book's website, there is a template (with behavior charts and graphs) for you to carry out your own projects. Good luck!

Before going on, try this brief quiz.

Quiz 10

1. If we say that a child speaks softly because she is shy, this is an example of a _____ explanation because the only evidence for her shyness is that she speaks softly.

2. True or False? Children are born with traits such as shyness.

_____

3. If a child cries when placed in his crib and the parent lets him out of the crib and the crying increases under similar circumstances, then letting him out of the crib is probably a _____ reinforcer for crying.

4. If your child says "No" when you ask her to do something, you should _____ the behavior of saying no and not let her out of having to do what you ask.

5. If you have more than one child, you can enlist _____ children to help provide positive reinforcement to the _____ children.

6. In the example of the little boy who tattled on his older siblings, when his parents started planned ignoring, another behavior emerged — telling his siblings how to do things — and this phenomenon is called _____.

7. True or False? The most effective way to get your kids to say "please" and "thank you" is to tell them and continue to remind them. _____

8. With very young children, the parents must show the child what to do or say. This is called _____.

9. Then, after showing them what to do or say, the parent should _____ the behavior. For example, in the case of saying "please" and "thank you," they could ask, "What do you say?"

10. Modeling and prompting behavior are only effective if the parents remember to _____*ly* _____ the behavior they want.

Quiz 10 Answers

1. If we say that a child speaks softly because she is shy, this is an example of a *circular* explanation because the only evidence for her shyness is that she speaks softly.

2. True or False? Children are born with traits such as shyness. *False*

3. If a child cries when placed in his crib and the parent lets him out of the crib, and the crying increases under similar circumstances, then letting him out of the crib is probably a *negative* reinforcer for crying.

4. If your child says "No" when you ask her to do something, you should *ignore* the behavior of saying no and not let her out of having to do what you ask.

5. If you have more than one child, you can enlist *older* children to help provide positive reinforcement to the *younger* children.

6. In the example of the little boy who tattled on his older siblings, when his parents started planned ignoring, another behavior emerged — telling his siblings how to do things — and this phenomenon is called *resurgence*.

7. True or False? The most effective way to get your kids to say "please" and "thank you" is to tell them and continue to remind them. *False*

8. With very young children, the parents must show the child what to do or say, called *modeling*.

9. Then, after showing them what to do or say, the parent should *prompt* the behavior. For example, in the case of saying "please" and "thank you," they could ask, "What do you say?"

10. Modeling and prompting behavior are only effective if the parents remember to *positively reinforce* the behavior they want.

Part V – Special Behavior Problems

Chapter 11: Examples of Social Positive Reinforcement of Children's Behavior That Raise Special Concerns

As mentioned throughout this book, one common parenting mistake is that many parents unintentionally (and sometimes intentionally) attend to (positively reinforce) inappropriate or undesirable behaviors in their children. Sometimes the behaviors may not seem to be particularly problematic at the time but later turn out to be. Because of this, there are some behaviors that raise special concerns. Consider the following examples.

1. While walking, a 3-year-old child labeled as "accident prone" bumps into a table. The parent immediately says with concern, "Are you alright?"
2. An 11-year-old is concerned about her looks and tells her mother that she wishes she could die. The mother, obviously upset by this statement, says, "You don't know what you're saying. You're a beautiful girl. You know we love you very much. C'mon now, let's talk about it."
3. In the classroom, a 7-year-old keeps getting up out of his seat. Every time he does, the teacher immediately tells him, "Sit down, Julian!"
4. A 5-year-old hits her baby brother. The father immediately pulls her onto his lap and says, "That's not nice. How would you like it if someone bigger than you hit you?"
5. A 6-year-old doesn't like that his parents won't let him have two helpings of dessert, so he screams and throws

a glass on the floor. His parents immediately ask, "Why did you do that?" and then give him another helping.

6. When a parent says "No" to an 8-year-old or scolds him, he begins to pout and hold his head down. Feeling bad, his mother asks him what's wrong, and the child says sternly, "Nothing's wrong!" Feeling even worse, the mother tries to talk to her son, asking "Are you alright?" But he goes to his room and slams the door.

In all of these examples, the behavior of a child is followed immediately by the social attention of an adult (and, in the case of #5, giving the child want he wants). Mostly, in these examples, the adult talks to the child immediately after the questionable behavior.

The question we need to ask is: What effect does the adult's attention have upon the child's behavior in the future, that is, under similar circumstances? And in such cases, there is a clue to the answer: these behavioral episodes between parent and child have probably happened before, often many times, and will most likely happen again unless or until the parent reacts differently. This means that the adult's behavior is probably functioning as a
_____ _____er for the child's behavior because the adult's attention is _____ immediately after the behavior and the child's behavior is _____ likely to occur under similar circumstances.

"But" you ask, "shouldn't adults talk to kids, especially if they're feeling bad or hurt?" "What's wrong with asking a child if he is all right after he bumps into a table?" "Why shouldn't a concerned parent talk to her daughter after the daughter makes a statement about wishing she could die?" "What's wrong with telling a child to sit down? After all, he is disrupting the classroom." "Why can't I have a talk with my child when she has just been aggressive toward her younger brother?" "Don't parents need to teach kids right from wrong?" "Why shouldn't parents ask their son why he threw a glass on the floor? He's obviously upset."

Let me answer all these questions in two ways. First, there is nothing inherently wrong with parents or teachers talking to children about inappropriate behaviors or how they're feeling. But,

if the adult's talking comes immediately after the child's behavior *and* the child tends to act in the same way under similar circumstances, then the adult's talking is functioning as a
_____ _____*er*. That means the adult is inadvertently strengthening the very behavior they don't want to occur. It's like the adult is saying to the child, "Do it again" ("Bump into tables again" or "Say you wish you would die again"). Of course, those are the last things parents want their children to do. Also, remember that the child doesn't know that his behavior is being reinforced; he is not doing these things consciously.

As I have said, you need to look at the effect of an outcome on the future behavior to see whether it is indeed a positive reinforcer. Let's look at the examples again in more detail in terms of what the adults did and what they could have done differently.

1. While walking, a 3-year-old child labeled as "accident prone" bumps into a table. The parent immediately says with concern, "Are you alright?"

If the child is not getting much attention from the parent at the time but immediately gets attention for bumping into the table, the child may unknowingly learn new ways to hurt himself and become increasingly "accident prone."

Plus, some kids not only learn such behaviors, but they learn to "feel" pain even though there is very little real pain. No-tear (reinforced) crying is often a sure giveaway that the pain is not real. Many parents are suckers for a little injury and dote on their kids under such circumstances. Conversely, many parents feel guilty for ignoring expressions of hurt, pain, or even throwing tantrums, especially when the behavior gets worse immediately. They feel this way because they think their kids are hurt or upset.

Does this mean that parents and teachers should never show concern when children hurt themselves? Of course not. But it should probably be reserved for injuries that are truly harmful and painful. And parents should be aware of the behavior that results in the injury and whether it occurs again and how often. Parents and teachers need to think about these things all the time. In other words, you need to be aware of your child's behaviors, the consequences, and whether the behaviors occur more or less often.

> 2. An 11-year-old is upset about her looks and tells her mother that she wishes she could die. The mother, obviously upset by this statement, says, "You don't know what you're saying. You're a beautiful girl. You know we love you very much. C'mon now, let's talk about it."

This is not a simple situation, especially in light of the growing incidence of childhood suicide. I can hear you asking now, "How can I not talk to my child when she expresses a wish to die?" However, remembering what effects social positive reinforcement can have, we have to ask ourselves whether the child really knows what she is saying and whether she really means it. I know this is tough, but consider the alternative. Talking to the child after such statements may actually reinforce these and similar statements. That means the parent may actually cause the child to talk (and think) more about dying, which, among other things, will make her feel worse about herself. Plus, remembering the effects of ignoring on positively reinforced behavior, think about what would happen if the parents reinforced the behavior frequently over a period of time and then decided to use planned ignoring. Remember that the behavior would immediately get worse, and this might lead the child to actually do something more than talk about dying — and that would be something you couldn't ignore.

It is possible that some kids say such things simply because they get the attention of adults, that is, the behaviors are reinforced. This doesn't mean that the kids say these things consciously. Remember, we are rarely, if ever, conscious that our behaviors are being reinforced or how. But it is also possible that some kids really do feel so bad that they think (talk to themselves) about dying. It is up to adults to try to distinguish between the two — not always an easy task.

Suppose that you don't immediately acknowledge what the child said, but instead look for more positive self-statements, or at least statements about her bad feelings that don't involve dying, and then attend to those. Or suppose you wait until a later time, and ask her, without acknowledging her previous statement, about the circumstances that you think are making her feel bad about herself. Even then, you need to be aware of how the conversation is going and what self-statements you might be reinforcing. The point of this example is not to tell you how to handle every such instance, but to make you aware of how you need to think about these situations to avoid inadvertently positively reinforcing undesirable and even self-destructive behaviors.

Also, it is important to note that we don't build a child's self-esteem by telling her she is beautiful, smart, and wonderful, but instead by reinforcing competent and successful behaviors.

3. In the classroom, a 7-year-old keeps getting up out of his seat. Every time he does, the teacher immediately tells him, "Sit down, Julian!"

This example is played out in thousands of classrooms all over the country every day. First of all, young children are naturally active, impulsive, distractible, and curious. When we send them to school, we make them sit for long periods of time in classrooms that are often boring. Moreover, if there are 20 or more children in a classroom and one teacher, it is often impossible for the teacher to attend to each child's appropriate behavior. Against this backdrop, a child who gets up out of his seat or talks to his neighbor will likely get the teacher's immediate attention (not to mention that of his or her classmates). So, teachers spend a considerable amount of classroom time saying, "Sit down!" "Pay attention!" "Stop that!" "Be quiet!"

The problem is that the teachers' comments, occurring as they do immediately after the inappropriate behaviors, often act as _____ _____ers for the behaviors. They actually cause the behaviors to increase. "But why," you ask, "would teachers knowingly make the problem worse?" There are two answers to that question. First, the teachers are not knowingly doing that; they are trying their best to maintain an orderly classroom. And second, the behaviors of yelling are themselves reinforced. Almost every time a teacher says, "Sit down," the child sits down — only to get up again. And almost every time a teacher yells, "Be quiet!" the child quiets down — only to talk again. And so on. Because the child's behavior of getting out of his seat is positively reinforced, and the teacher's behavior of yelling is negatively reinforced, it's a vicious cycle that both the teacher and student are caught in.

As you learned in Chapters 6 and 7, there are three alternatives to reinforcing undesirable behavior: 1) planned ignoring of the undesirable behavior, 2) positive reinforcement of a different but desirable behavior, and 3) punishment.

Using the combination of planned ignoring of the undesirable behavior and (positive) reinforcement for a different but desirable behavior is preferred. So, when a child stands up, the teacher, having already decided what behaviors to target, ignores the behavior, *and* when the teacher observes the child sitting quietly, the teacher uses social positive reinforcement, by simply talking to the child or by using specific praise such as, "Julian, I really like the way you're sitting in your seat and being quiet. That's great!"

Of course, teachers can also incorporate a token system, whereby children get a token or a point for being in their seat at a certain time and lose a token or point when the teacher observes them getting out of their seat without permission. In other words, there is more than one way to use positive reinforcement to get the desired behavior.

4. A 5-year-old hits her baby brother. The father immediately pulls her onto his lap and says, "That's not nice. How would you like it if someone bigger than you hit you?"

Most parents think, correctly, that it is their job to teach their children right from wrong. But most parents think, incorrectly, that the best way to do this is to reason with them.

Although such a strategy may work for some older kids (and I would argue that, just as with adults, it probably doesn't most of the time), it has many risks with younger children. I often see parents on their knees reasoning with 2- or 3-year-old children, and they usually do this immediately after the child has engaged in some inappropriate behavior. "When else should a parent reason with a young child about right and wrong?" you ask.

Think about the above example from the 5-year-old's perspective. She hits her baby brother, and immediately she gets to sit on Dad's lap and get his undivided attention. If she could reason (talk to herself about it), it would be easy for her to assume that she only gets such attention for hitting her baby brother. Having learned about positive reinforcement, you now know that, instead of teaching her right from wrong, the father may be teaching her the very behavior he doesn't want her to perform.

What could he do as an alternative? Well, for starters he could use planned ignoring for the hitting behavior, assuming it's not very severe, *and* try to notice when she is playing nicely, sharing, and cooperating with her baby brother, and then pick her up and sit her on his lap. Using specific praise, he could say, "_____."

Some have even suggested that in such situations, the parent attend to the child who is hit. Or if ignoring the hitting behavior is not an option because of the burst that might occur, then the father could teach his daughter more acceptable ways of interacting with her brother. He could do this by using what is known as Behavioral Skills Training (see Chapter 13).

5. A 6-year-old doesn't like that his parents won't let him have two helpings of dessert, so he screams and throws a glass on the floor. His parents immediately ask, "Why did you do that?" and then give him another helping.

Some people believe, probably rightly so, that it is a good idea to allow children to express their emotions. But there are some forms of emotional expression that are not acceptable. Throwing things, yelling at others, using profanity, and crying at the slightest little thing are just some of the forms of expression that may not be appropriate. However, it is just these forms that we often positively reinforce because they are attention-getters.

As in some of the other examples, the parents in this example should probably have used planned ignoring for the screaming and glass-throwing and looked for some more appropriate form of expression such as the 6-year-old saying, "I'm upset that you won't let me have dessert." The parents could then say, "We know and understand, but one helping is enough and you can have one tomorrow night," or something like this. Of course, the parents would need to look at the future effect of saying these things to their son to make sure they weren't positively reinforcing too much complaining that they wouldn't let him have dessert. Also, parents need to make sure that they don't get into a debate about it. They can explain their reasoning once and then ignore any further attempts to talk about it.

Unfortunately, by the time kids get to the point where they are screaming and throwing things, using planned ignoring can have potentially harmful effects, because, as you already know, when we withhold a positive reinforcer from a behavior, the behavior immediately _____. In this example, using planned ignoring may result in a burst in which more things are thrown and broken, behaviors that are much more difficult to ignore. In such cases, the parents would need to use an alternative such as time-out from positive reinforcement for throwing the tantrum.

6. When a parent says "No" to an 8-year-old or scolds him, he begins to pout and hold his head down. Feeling bad, his mother asks him what's wrong, and the child says sternly, "Nothing's wrong!" Feeling even worse, the mother tries to talk to her son, asking "Are you alight?" But he goes to his room and slams the door.

Unlike the behaviors in the previous example, which may be called aggressive, the behaviors in this example (pouting, answering "Nothing's wrong," and going to the room and slamming the door) may be called *passive aggressive*. They are called that because they have a similar effect on the parent as aggression, but without the direct confrontation. They are much more subtle forms of aggression. But why do they occur?

First, many children learn to behave in a passive aggressive way from parents who behave in such ways. In other words, the child models the behavior of the parent in similar circumstances (see Appendix I). The question we must ask is: what effect do those behaviors have on the parent? In this example, the child's passive aggressive behaviors cause the parent to feel bad and then to pay attention to them by asking "What's wrong?" and "Are you alright?" The more the parent talks to the child, the more the child behaves passive aggressively. That's what such behaviors are designed to do: make you feel bad.

By now, you should have figured out that the solution is to not pay attention to those behaviors, and to wait until other, more appropriate behaviors occur to pay attention to. In this example, it might be more appropriate for the child to be more assertive with his parent, for example, by saying something like "I don't like it when you yell at me." This behavior is a preferable alternative to the passive aggressive behaviors. And the parent may want to reinforce it by saying something like "I understand that you don't like it, but I didn't like what you did." Of course, the parent must always be vigilant about reinforcing too much. For example, in this instance, you don't want to get into a long, drawn-out discussion where you answer everything your child says (see Appendix I).

As you can see, it is very difficult to avoid reinforcing undesirable behaviors because, as noted previously, we all operate on automatic pilot. We don't really think about what we're doing in every situation or at every moment. One goal of this book is to help you practice becoming aware not only of your child's behavior, but also of yours.

It is also very difficult to use positive reinforcement in a planned and prudent manner. It takes a lot of vigilance to notice all your child's behaviors and to decide which behaviors are to be ignored and which are to be positively reinforced. However, if you can make these distinctions, you can prevent many problem behaviors — and make you and your child happy about your relationship.

Before going on, try this brief quiz.

Quiz 11

1. In all the examples in this chapter, the behavior of a child is followed by social _____ of an adult.

2. If the child's behavior increases under similar circumstances, then the social attention of the adult is most likely functioning as a _____ _____er for the child's behavior.

3. True or False? Parents should never talk to their children about their bad behavior. _____

4. It is possible that the behaviors (bumping into things, etc.) that get a child labeled as "accident prone" may simply have been _____ by the attention they get from parents and others.

5. It is also possible that children may learn behaviors that result in injury because they produce the parents' social _____.

6. True or False? When a very young child talks about killing himself, he has probably not really thought it out carefully and does not really understand what death is. _____

7. Children's misbehavior in classrooms usually occurs because it is followed by attention from teachers and peers, which functions as _____ _____ because those behaviors increase, or are strengthened, under similar circumstances (when they are in the classroom).

8. True or False? Reasoning with very young children is usually a good way to get them to understand what you want them to do or not do. _____

9. True or False? It is not a good idea to use planned ignoring for aggressive, destructive behaviors. _____

10. Behaviors, such as pouting and slamming doors, that make others feel bad without directly confronting them are called _____ aggressive.

Quiz 11 Answers

1. In all the examples in this chapter, the behavior of a child is followed by social *attention* of an adult.

2. If the child's behavior increases under similar circumstances, then the social attention of the adult is most likely functioning as a *positive reinforcer* for the child's behavior.

3. True or False? Parents should never talk to their children about their bad behavior. *False*

4. It is possible that the behaviors (bumping into things, etc.) that get a child labeled as "accident prone" may simply have been *reinforced* by the attention they get from parents and others.

5. It is also possible that children may learn behaviors that result in injury because they produce the parents' social *attention*.

6. True or False? When a very young child talks about killing himself, he has probably not really thought it out carefully and does not really understand what death is. *True*

7. Children's misbehavior in classrooms usually occurs because it is followed by attention from teachers and peers, which functions as *positive reinforcement* because those behaviors increase, or are strengthened, under similar circumstances (when they are in the classroom).

8. True or False? Reasoning with very young children is usually a good way to get them to understand what you want them to do or not do. *False*

9. True or False? It is not a good idea to use planned ignoring for aggressive, destructive behaviors. *True*

10. Behaviors, such as pouting and slamming doors, that make others feel bad without directly confronting them are called *passive* aggressive.

Chapter 12: How to Deal with Some Specific Behavioral Problems

Throughout this book, I have tried to teach you a general problem-solving strategy when it comes to children's behavior. What that means is that no matter what behavioral problem you encounter, you should be able to solve it with the methods presented in this book. In this chapter, however, I will describe four specific behavioral problems and some evidence-based solutions to give you an idea how some behavioral scientists and practitioners have tackled these problems with the tools described in Chapters 3-7.

The following examples illustrate some research-based strategies for specific problems. Let's begin with sleep problems.

Bedtime Resistance

One of the most common problems parents deal with is "bedtime resistance," which may include crying and getting out of bed at night. Let's face it, unless you take the steps recommended in Chapter 13 to prevent bedtime resistance, you will need some strategies to deal with that problem. In Chapters 13 and 14, I describe two examples of how parents have dealt with different sleep problems in a 4-month-old and a 2 ½-year-old. Here I will describe a technique that can be used with somewhat older children, called the "bedtime pass," based on positive reinforcement and planned ignoring.

To use this technique, you make a laminated 5 x 7 card with the child's name on it (actually, the card doesn't really have to be laminated or 5 x 7; it's up to you). The child is told beforehand — not when they cry and get out of bed — that they can use the pass for 1 visit out of their room after bedtime (For younger children, you can start with a pass for 2 times out of the room.). The bedtime pass can be used with kids from approximately 3 to 10 years of age.

When you discuss the bedtime pass with your child, you tell them that the pass can only be used for short visits and for specific purposes, such as getting a drink or going to the bathroom or for a hug, but not more than about 2-3 minutes. Following the visit, the child must give the pass back to the parent until the next night. If the child cries or leaves the room again, which you should probably expect, you should ignore those behaviors and return the child to the room with little or no attention. Remember, do not explain any more about the pass or say that she should not cry and needs to stay in her bed. That will only add attention to, and possible positively reinforce, the inappropriate behaviors.

Consistent with the general approach in this book, you might want to count the behaviors — the number of times a night the child gets out bed and, possibly, the duration of crying — for about a week before you begin to use the pass. Be sure to graph these so you can tell whether the bedtime pass is really working.

Saying Bad Words

Most parents can't wait for their children to start talking, that is, until they start talking back, saying "no" to everything, and maybe worst of all, uttering those dreaded four-letter words. Although this section is about saying bad words, a note about saying "no" is in order.

The first thing to understand is that there is no stage when all kids start saying "no." If you think about it, saying "no" is a powerful behavior because, for such a little word, it can have powerful effects. So, when a child first says "no" and it works to stop the parent from doing something, it doesn't take much more than a single reinforcement for it to begin to occur more often. So, if you don't want your toddler to say "no" a lot, don't let it work so well.

Now, to saying bad words. The question is: What can parents do to prevent their little tykes from sounding like sailors?

The first step: Set a good example. In other words, be a good model (see also Appendix I). Children learn the words they use by hearing others use them. If you use four-letter words under certain circumstances, such as when you are angry or frustrated, then you model those words for your child and shouldn't be surprised if she repeats them and uses them under similar circumstances (when she is angry or frustrated). Behavioral psychologists know enough about modeling and imitation to suggest that the old adage that I heard from my parents when I was a child, "Do as I say, not as I do," doesn't usually work.

But, you say, "I never curse, and my little princess still uttered a bad word." Unfortunately, you can't control what she hears from others. As many parents know, even if you never allow your children to hear swear words at home, they will likely hear them at school. Nowadays, 2- and 3-year-old children are showing up at daycare or preschool already sophisticated at the art of swearing.

The second step: Plan ahead for the almost inevitable curse word. Know exactly what you will do when your child utters the unutterable. And, of course, what you should do is ignore the bad word and positively reinforce any other, more acceptable words.

Try not to be caught off-guard, or you will miss the opportunity to take full advantage of step three: Immediately ignore the behavior. Do not look at your child, do not chide or scold her, and do not sit her down and explain why such words are not allowed in your house.

The reason you should ignore the behavior is that if children notice that a particular word gets immediate attention from their parents, they will likely continue to utter it, even if they are oblivious to the word's meaning. The fact that they continue to utter the bad word means that the attention you gave them is a _____ _____ er. They don't know it's a bad word until the parent reacts dramatically. And for most children, that is pretty entertaining.

But you ask, "How will my child ever learn she's not supposed to say these words if I don't sit her down and explain it?" Let me reiterate what I said in Chapter 5: If you don't pay attention to those words, your child will stop saying them. And that is how she will learn they are not acceptable. If you absolutely have to reason with your child, then do it at another time when she hasn't just uttered the bad word. That way she won't see cursing as a way to get your immediate, undivided attention.

Also, remember to pay attention to your child when she utters more acceptable words in the face of frustration or anger. If you use alternative words when you are angry or frustrated, you increase the chances that your child will also use them when she is angry or frustrated.

Interruptions

All parents reinforce their children for talking — some a lot! In fact, some children constantly interrupt their parents (and others) when they're talking on the phone or in person to another adult or a sibling.

Why do some kids interrupt? Because they are rude, right? No. Remember that would be a faulty circular explanation because the only evidence for their rudeness is that they interrupt. And as you might be able to guess, the parents are responsible for their kids' interruptions because they unknowingly reinforce them. But how do parents unknowingly teach their kids to interrupt? Simple. By allowing the interruption to actually work, that is, to get the parents to stop their conversation and pay attention to the child.

So how can we deal with those interruptions?

We can start by teaching young children not to interrupt. Almost as soon as they learn to talk fluently, young children begin interrupting adult conversations; they don't know any better. After all, we have always listened to them and reinforced their talking up to this point (Remember that the kid is always right.). A common time for young children to interrupt is when we're on the phone. Sometimes we try to ignore their interruptions, but they immediately become louder and go on longer (the burst when reinforced behavior is ignored). So, we give in and either end our call or tell the person on the other end of the line to hold on, which, of course, probably _____s the interruption.

You can teach your youngsters not to interrupt and to wait until you're finished with your conversation by first modeling such behavior for them. After all, it's not fair for you to interrupt and then not allow them to interrupt. The first time they try to interrupt, you should say to them "Please wait until I'm finished," but — and this is important — make sure you finish after only a few seconds. Then you should thank (praise) them for waiting and listen to what they wanted to tell you. Over time, gradually lengthen the period they must wait until it equals the length of your conversations. But always go to them, praise them for waiting, and ask them what they wanted to say. If they try to interrupt during this process, you must ignore the interruption and its inevitable rise in volume (the burst) when your child realizes that you will not pay attention to her.

Remember, just because your children say, "Excuse me," doesn't automatically mean they get to interrupt. As parents know, young children will say "excuse me" over and over again because it has worked in the past to get you to stop what you're doing and listen to them.

Reading Books or Screen Time?

According to the Kaiser Family Foundation (https://www.kff.org/other/poll-finding/report-generation-m2-media-in-the-lives/), kids ages 8 to 18 now spend an average of 7.5 hours in front of a screen each day (not including for school), 4.5 of which are spent watching TV. By contrast, the average amount of time American children age 6 and under spend reading or being read to daily is only 41 minutes.

With strong competition from television, video games, smart phones, and tablets, plus after-school activities and homework, it's no wonder that American children don't spend much time reading books.

It is possible, however, to get your children to read more without depriving them of the luxuries of technology. First, remember that as a parent you're always a model. If, from very early on, your children see you reading and discussing what you read in an interesting, excited manner, they will be more likely to model that. Second, you should always make books available to your children from the time they are born and be prepared to notice any interest your child shows in reading — including comic books, magazines, etc. — and reinforce their behavior of reading by talking with them.

You can also get your child to read more by setting up a reading program (Remember the example in Chapter 9?). Start with a brief (10- to 15-minute) request to read. You can give your child a choice of what to read with some veto power. But remember, children are more likely to be interested in what they choose to read rather than what you choose for them.

Make sure your child reads in a distraction-free location. To help him (and you) remember how much time has passed, place a portable timer where both of you can hear it when it rings. You can tell him that he may read more but no less than the allotted time. To ensure that your child actually reads, you will need to talk to him about it, either by asking questions or allowing him to summarize what he read. Don't just go through the motions; be genuinely interested. Many parents find it useful to have their children read before going to bed at night. In fact, that can be a family rule starting when they're infants (see Chapter 14) and you read to them at bedtime.

Arrange some rewards for your child's reading. Problems may arise when your child wants to watch TV or play video games instead. If this happens, the situation calls for the use of Grandma's Rule: allowing a child to engage in a preferred activity (like TV watching) *only* if he first engages in a less preferred activity (in this case, reading).

After your child is regularly reading for at least 10 or 15 minutes a day, you can extend it to 20 minutes for a week or so, and then 30 minutes, etc. Remember to be consistent. If you allow your child to watch TV without reading, he'll assume — with good reason — that he can get away with it again. Also, if you show less interest in his video games and television shows, and more interest in what he's reading, he may begin to spend more time reading.

If you follow this plan, your child will read more and hopefully learn to love it. Incredibly, he may actually come to prefer it to his technological toys.

Before going on, try this brief quiz.

Quiz 12

1. Sleep problems, such as getting out of bed and calling out to the parents, are called bedtime _____.

2. A laminated card with the child's name on it that he or she can use to get out of bed one time (or two in very young children) a night is called a bedtime _____.

3. The best strategy to use when your child utters her first bad word is to _____ it.

4. True or False? A child will understand not to say bad words if you just reason with her and tell her why it's not okay. _____

5. True or False? A child will understand not to say bad words if you ignore whenever she says a bad word. _____

6. True or False? Children interrupt their parents because the kids are rude and don't have manners. _____

7. The best way to teach your child not to interrupt is to start by asking them to wait a _____ period of time while you finish your other conversation and then immediately turn to the child and allow them to tell you what they wanted to say.

8. True or False? Just because your child says, "Excuse me," doesn't automatically mean they get to interrupt. _____

9. If you want your child to read, you should always _____ the behavior of reading yourself.

10. In addition to modeling the behavior yourself, you can _____*ly* _____ the behavior of reading.

Quiz 12 Answers

1. Sleep problems, such as getting out of bed and calling out to the parents, are called *bedtime resistance*.

2. A laminated card with the child's name on it that he or she can use to get out of bed one time (or two in very young children) a night is called a bedtime *pass*.

3. The best strategy to use when your child utters her first bad word is to *ignore* it.

4. True or False? A child will understand not to say bad words if you just reason with her and tell her why it's not okay. *False*

5. True or False? A child will understand not to say bad words if you ignore whenever she says a bad word. *True*

6. True or False? Children interrupt their parents because the kids are rude and don't have manners. *False*

7. The best way to teach your child not to interrupt is to start by asking them to wait a *short* period of time while you finish your other conversation and then immediately turn to the child and allow her to tell you what she wanted to say.

8. True or False? Just because your child says, "Excuse me," doesn't automatically mean they get to interrupt. *True*

9. If you want your child to read, you should always model the behavior of *reading* yourself.

10. In addition to modeling the behavior yourself, you can *positively reinforce* the behavior of reading.

Part VI – Preventing Bad Behavior and Teaching Your Infant

Chapter 13: Preventing Bad Behavior by Building Good Behavior Early in Life

They say that an ounce of prevention is worth a pound of cure, and that couldn't be any truer for raising kids. Many of the behaviors I have used as examples in this book have been problem behaviors. In other words, they are behaviors that parents (and others) have inadvertently reinforced and want to decrease or change in some other way. In short, the kids have already learned to exhibit undesirable behaviors.

Early on in the book, I stated that parents make two general kinds of errors: They inadvertently reinforce bad behavior, and they fail to reinforce good behavior. The point of this chapter is that you can prevent most undesirable behaviors from ever occurring if you positively reinforce desirable alternative behaviors. In other words, **the more you positively reinforce good, desirable, appropriate behaviors, the less you will have to deal with bad, undesirable, inappropriate behaviors.** The phrase "Catch them being good" is apropos. In this chapter, I will offer a few examples of the many behaviors that can be reinforced (taught) and that will prevent bad behaviors from occurring.

Sleeping Alone

Perhaps the biggest problem parents have with their children involves sleep, in particular, what is referred to as *bedtime resistance* (see Chapter 12), which often includes crying, calling out from or leaving the bedroom, or climbing into the parents' bed.

Consider the following example: A 2 ½-year-old would get out of her bed in the middle of the night and slip into her mother's bed. When the daughter was returned to her own bed, she would scream and cry, at which point the mother would either go into the daughter's room to check on her or let her back into her bed, the latter because it stopped the screaming and crying — a negative reinforcer for the mother's behavior of letting her back into her bed. The mother's behaviors of attending to her daughter and letting her sleep in her bed were positive reinforcers for her daughter's behaviors.

Because these bedtime resistance behaviors are not pleasant for parents who usually must get up early for work and to get their kids ready for school, the parents often do what's easy. This frequently means either having a parent sleep in the child's room or allowing the child to sleep in the parents' bed. These behaviors by the parents are negatively reinforced because the crying immediately stops (is subtracted).

Bedtime resistance behaviors can be prevented with some simple steps, which are admittedly not that simple in practice with your own child.

To begin with, you need to know that the ultimate goal is for the child to sleep alone without incident in his own room. How can you ensure your child will do this? You will have to build the behavior, and it is helpful to begin very early. In fact, you can start with newborns, but there are some considerations. First, the infant's room must be right next to or very near the parents' room. Second, it is helpful if the parents have the infant on a feeding schedule, for example, once every few hours during the night. That way if the infant cries you know it's not because she's hungry. Third, before you put her to bed, you must make sure she is comfortable and not in pain. Fourth, it's always a good idea to have a sleep routine that is the same every night and that happens at about the same time. It could include getting ready (putting on pajamas, brushing teeth for older children) and reading to your infant or young child. You might lie in bed with them for a few minutes talking before you leave the room.

The fifth step is the hardest because it involves leaving the room. If your infant or child cries, which is very likely, you should go back in with as little fanfare as possible and check to make sure she is alright, then leave the room and don't go back in. She will likely continue to cry and may even cry louder and longer. (This is the burst of behavior that occurs when behavior does not produce reinforcement.) The hardest part is not going back into the room when she is crying. But you should know that you are not being mean or neglectful. You should also know that the infant is not sad or unhappy. Eventually she will fall asleep, and you will be pleasantly surprised that when she awakens in the morning, she will be cheerful, and the incident will be forgotten. If you are consistent and follow the same procedure every night, the crying will stop sooner, until your infant will not cry at all when you put her to bed.

Of course, if you put your infant to bed and she doesn't cry, then you should make sure you provide attention for that. You don't have to specifically praise it like you might for an older child, but just paying attention to your infant by talking to and caressing her will probably suffice as positive reinforcement for being quiet in bed.

If you don't want to ignore the crying with a very young infant, that is fine; but you will have to do it eventually. And the longer you wait, the more likely it is that some bedtime resistance behaviors will emerge. The bottom line is: *Make sure you do not pay attention to bedtime resistance behaviors, and make sure you do positively reinforce bedtime compliance behaviors.*

By the way, in the example at the beginning of this section, the mother was able to decrease the bedtime resistance behaviors (see Chapter 12 for another solution for dealing with this problem) by using planned ignoring for both the behaviors of her daughter getting into bed with her and of throwing a tantrum when she was placed back in her own bed. As expected, the tantrum behavior initially increased — a burst — but the mother was consistent, and both behaviors decreased. Also, in the morning, if the little girl had stayed in her bed, the mother would use specific praise ("I'm really proud of you for sleeping in your own bed. You're a big girl now."). At the end of the project, the little girl slept in her own bed every night and no longer tried to get into bed with her mother. Both were much happier as a result.

But wouldn't it have been much easier to build good sleep behaviors in the first place, so the mother didn't have to deal with bedtime resistance?

Playing Nicely

Some kids do not play nicely. They grab toys from other kids or siblings. They hit, kick, bite, or pull the hair of other kids during playtime. They cry and scream when they aren't allowed to play with a toy or engage in a desired activity. And so on. Some people might say that kids engage in these behaviors because they are spoiled, aggressive, selfish, etc. But you should recognize these as faulty circular explanations. Remember, you must ask what evidence there is that the child is aggressive or selfish or spoiled, and if the only evidence is the very behaviors you want to explain, then those explanations are circular and don't explain the behavior at all. Based on what we've discussed in this book, however, you should know that these behaviors continue to occur because they are _____*ed* in some way.

But how are they reinforced? In order to answer that question, you would have to observe what happens immediately after each behavior occurs. For example, in a typical preschool setting, when one child hits, bites, or pulls the hair of another child, teachers often pay immediate attention to that child, usually by explaining why it is not appropriate behavior. However, as you might guess, that attention probably inadvertently positively reinforces the bad behavior. It is positive because the attention is _____, and it is a reinforcer because the bad behavior is _____ likely to occur under similar circumstances. Remember, reasoning with a very young child doesn't work. And if it occurs immediately after some undesirable behavior, it may reinforce that behavior, which means it may be _____ likely to occur again under similar circumstances.

Parents or teachers can prevent such behavior in the first place by positively reinforcing behaviors of playing nicely. The first thing to do is to define what we mean by playing nicely. In other words, what behaviors comprise what we would call playing nicely? These might include such behaviors as asking for a toy instead of grabbing it, or giving a toy to another child when he or she asks for it, or perhaps picking up a toy that another kid dropped.

The second thing to do is to arrange for the behavior to occur. There are several ways to do this depending on whether the child has already been observed to engage in the behavior. If you have observed, or do observe, the child engaging in the behavior, you should immediately _____*ly* _____ the behavior by delivering specific praise, such as saying, "Luke, I really like the way you gave the truck to Taia when she asked for it" and/or giving a high five, etc.

If you have never observed the child doing the behavior, then you can build the behavior. The first step is to give a simple instruction, such as "Luke, please give the truck to Taia to play with." If Luke gives the truck to Taia, then you should deliver some specific praise, such as "Good job giving Taia the truck when I asked you to do so."

If a simple instruction doesn't work, the next step is to model the behavior and then have the child do the same behavior. In this example, you would take the truck and give it to Taia and then ask Luke to do the same followed by specific praise. It is also possible that you may need to physically prompt Luke to give the truck to Taia by physically moving Luke's hands with the truck to Taia and then providing specific praise. Then, you would keep doing that while gradually fading your physical prompt until Luke can do it alone.

The method described above is called *Behavioral Skills Training* (BST) and can be used in teaching a wide variety of skills. Notice that it consists of four general steps in a specific order: 1) instructing the child how to behave; 2) modeling the correct behavior yourself; 3) role playing, that is, having the child do the behavior; and 4) giving feedback in the form of specific praise or some other consequence that will hopefully function as a reinforcer.

You can teach appropriate behavior as a way to prevent inappropriate behavior from occurring. When you decide to build the behavior, you have to decide ahead of time what behaviors are appropriate under which circumstances. Then you arrange the circumstance and teach the appropriate behavior, always remembering to positively reinforce the behavior when it occurs.

For example, it is almost universally appropriate for children to comply with their parents' requests. So, start asking your kids to do what you want as early as possible and help them learn how to do it using BST. It is recommended that you start simple: request a behavior that you know the child can do and that does not require a lot of effort. Remember the instruction ("Please pick up the toy") is given first. Then wait to see what the child does. If she does not pick up the toy within a few seconds, then go to the next steps in the BST method: modeling it for her and then having her do it. Remember, *the most important part is to reinforce the behavior of doing what you ask.*

Doing What I Ask You to Do

Speaking of compliance, not complying with parents' requests or demands is one of the biggest problems parents face with their children. In fact, some behaviors are so bad (notice that I didn't say the kids are bad), that there is an official diagnosis for them: Oppositional Defiant Disorder (ODD). Kids diagnosed with ODD are said to be uncooperative, defiant, and hostile toward peers, parents, teachers, and other authority figures. Unfortunately, such descriptions do not specify exactly what behaviors are observed. However, it's a good guess that kids diagnosed with ODD not only do not comply with parental requests or demands, but they may also say "No!" argue, scream, cry, or throw things when asked to do something.

You should know that I don't believe that these kids have anything wrong with them. That is, they don't *have* a disorder (whatever that means). Just as kids who frequently get up out of their seats in the classroom and have trouble paying attention to the teacher don't *have* a disorder called ADHD. Both of these so-called disorders are simply names for a collection of behaviors under certain circumstances. They don't explain the behaviors. Remember our adage from earlier in the book: *The kid is always right.* What this means isn't that the kid does the right behavior, but rather that the behaviors are caused. And based on the approach in this book, the primary causes of the behaviors lie in the environment, specifically the consequences for such behaviors.

It's a good bet that the child who doesn't comply with requests engages in behaviors such as crying, screaming, or throwing things and that those behaviors are reinforced. Before I talk about how to get your kids to do what you ask, let's try to figure out what the reinforcers might be for non-compliance. To do that, simply imagine a situation in which a parent asks a child to do something and the child screams "No!" and then maybe cries and begins to throw a tantrum. Think about what you would do. For most parents, having a child scream and cry or throw a tantrum is very unpleasant, especially if those behaviors occur in public. Moreover, the parents can escape from that unpleasantness by removing the request. So, if a parent asks a child to clean his room or do his homework and the child screams and cries, the parent might say, "Okay, you don't have to do it now." So, the parent escapes from the crying and screaming, and the parent's behavior of removing the request is _____*ly* reinforced because something is subtracted or taken away — the crying and screaming — and the parent is more likely to remove requests under similar circumstances in the future. Likewise, the child's behavior of screaming and crying is also _____*ly* reinforced because as soon as they start crying and screaming, the parent removes or subtracts the request. The result is that both parent and child will continue the same behaviors in the future. They don't know it, but they are both reinforcing each other's behaviors. These types of interactions are often the basis of much worse behaviors by the child, which escalate and are associated with a range of problems later in life, such as aggression and anti-social behaviors (see Appendix I).

Of course, the parent might also try to reason with the child when he screams and cries, thus paying attention to the behaviors. In this case the child's behaviors may be _____*ly* reinforced because the parent's attention is added and the child will likely continue to cry and scream under similar circumstances. The bottom line for this discussion is that the child's ODD is nothing more than the behaviors that have been reinforced, usually over a long period of time until they become severe.

The solution is to prevent such behaviors in the first place, and it is pretty easy to do! First, you have to be ready to recognize the behavior when it happens. It might be as simple as the child putting a cup down when you ask him to. In such instances, be ready to use specific praise, such as "Thank you for doing what I asked," or "Thank you for putting the cup down when I asked you to," or "Good job doing what I asked!" There are many very simple compliant behaviors that you can watch for and positively reinforce.

If for some reason, your child doesn't comply with a simple request, you will have to build the behavior. You can start by making a simple request. It can be as simple as "Raise your arm," or "Point to the ball," or "Pick up the book," or "Give me the cup." If your child doesn't do what you ask, you can prompt the behavior, for example, by physically raising the child's arm when you ask the child to "Raise your arm" and saying "Good job!" Or you can put the book in the child's hand when you say "Pick up the book" and then say "Good job!" You can then gradually fade out your prompts until the child does what you ask without any help. You always want to start out simply and then gradually request more complex actions. Remember to make sure that you reinforce all compliance. For more complex requests, such as "Please clean up your room" or "Put your clothes away," you should start out simply and build the behavior from one item to many. Then you can vary the reinforcement to include activities (like 15 minutes of watching TV or playing video games, 30 minutes of playing outside, etc.) in addition to social attention.

If you start out very early in the child's life positively reinforcing and building compliance, you will have many fewer problems. Once again, if you accomplish this, both you and your child will feel good about each other and be happy. And the child's — and your — self-esteem will be high.

Before going on, try this brief quiz.

Quiz 13

1. Behaviors such as calling out to the parents or leaving the bedroom at night are called _____ resistance.

2. The ultimate goal with respect to sleep is for the child to sleep _____ without incident.

3. It is important to have a sleep _____ in which the child is put to bed at about the same time every night.

4. If your child engages in any sleep resistance behaviors when you leave the room, after checking on her without much fanfare, you should _____ those behaviors.

5. The bottom line is to make sure you do not pay _____ to bedtime resistance behaviors and do _____*ly* _____ bedtime compliance behaviors.

6. The simplest way to prevent inappropriate behaviors while playing with other children is to _____*ly* _____ behaviors we would call "playing nicely" or "sharing."

7. The method in which parents instruct children in what to do, then model the appropriate behavior and reinforce that behavior is called _____ _____ Training.

8. The official diagnosis for kids who are non-compliant is _____ _____ Disorder.

9. Because behaviors like crying and screaming get a kid out of having to do what is asked (the parental demands are subtracted), these behaviors are _____*ly* reinforced.

10. Of course, if the parents try to reason with a child when he or she is crying or screaming, that might _____*ly* reinforce such behaviors.

Quiz 13 Answers

1. Behaviors such as calling out to the parents or leaving the bedroom at night are called *bedtime resistance.*

2. The ultimate goal with respect to sleep is for the child to sleep *alone* without incident.

3. It is important to have a sleep *routine* in which the child is put to bed at about the same time every night.

4. If your child engages in any sleep resistance behaviors when you leave the room, after checking on her without much fanfare, you should *ignore* those behaviors.

5. The bottom line is to make sure you do not pay *attention* to bedtime resistance behaviors and do *positively reinforce* bedtime compliance behaviors.

6. The simplest way to prevent inappropriate behaviors while playing with other children is to *positively reinforce* behaviors we would call "playing nicely" or "sharing."

7. The method in which parents instruct children in what to do, then model the appropriate behavior and reinforce that behavior is call *Behavioral Skills* Training.

8. The official diagnosis for kids who are non-compliant is *Oppositional Defiant* Disorder.

9. Because behaviors like crying and screaming get a kid out of having to do what is asked (the parental demands are subtracted), these behaviors are *negatively reinforced.*

10. Of course, if the parents try to reason with a child when he or she is crying or screaming, that might *positively reinforce* such behavior.

Chapter 14: Teaching Your Infant

As a parent, you can begin teaching your child right after they are born. Moreover, you can even accelerate some, primarily motor, behaviors typically thought of as strictly maturational. In this chapter, I want to offer some general advice on what you might do, or not do, with your infant.

The first thing to know is that when babies are born, they have no purposeful, coordinated behavior. Such behavior must be built from the ground up. Much of it is built through interactions with the physical environment, as in the example of reaching and grasping discussed in Chapter 1. But some of the infant's behavioral repertoire is built through interactions with the parents and others, including siblings, relatives, and other care providers.

When Can I Start Teaching My Infant?

Parents frequently wonder if there's an age when their children are too young to learn. Unfortunately, many so-called experts give unscientific advice. For example, sometimes "experts" will say that a child can be potty trained or can sleep on their own only "when they're ready," implying that there is some sort of biological milestone that has to occur. Now it is true that children can't learn to talk until there is a certain development of their vocal musculature and they can't learn to walk until their legs are strong enough to support them. Other than obvious musculoskeletal or anatomical or physiological developments, no one really knows if there is a lower limit on learning. Consider the following examples of teaching very young infants and children.

Case 1: Roll Over, Baby

Typically, infants younger than 4 months of age are not yet rolling over on their own; in fact, some might say that they are not biologically ready. In this example, a mother used positive social reinforcement, consisting of specific praise (even though her daughter didn't understand what she was saying) and stroking the top of her head when her 4-month-old daughter made any movement from her back to her stomach. The mother then gradually looked for behaviors that were closer to the one behavior that would propel her over, for instance, using the foot on the opposite side to push her towards a toy. You might recognize the procedure the mother used as *shaping*, which is a way to build behaviors.

After just three weeks, the infant was rolling over several times a day. The number of successful attempts increased from zero during baseline to 24! This example is consistent with developmental research showing that enriching the environment and making it more reactive, in this case through the use of positive reinforcement, can result in behaviors occurring earlier than they would otherwise. Of course, There may or may not be any long-term benefit in learning to roll over, or even to walk, earlier, other than demonstrating the power of positive reinforcement.

Case 2: Sleep Through the Night

The mother of a 4-month-old wanted her infant to sleep through the night without crying. The mother knew her daughter wasn't hungry because she fed her on a schedule, and she knew that she wasn't in pain. Nevertheless, the infant would cry every night, and the mother would go in and breastfeed her.

To get her infant to sleep through the night, the mother used planned ignoring for the crying. Of course, it was difficult listening to her infant crying. Another problem arose because the father wanted to give in and go into the infant's room and quiet her down, which would have violated the rule of consistency (a problem faced in many families). So, the mother had to work on the behavior of two individuals, her infant and her husband. However, by the end of the project, the infant would quickly go to sleep when placed in bed, and the father had a better appreciation of the methods the mother used.

A Reactive Environment

Previously, I mentioned the concept of a reactive environment. Let me explain what I mean. We can talk about two kinds of environments, the *social* and the *nonsocial*, or *physical*. The social environment consists of other people, and the nonsocial consists of things and objects. For example, a smart phone is a perfect example of a nonsocial reactive environment. It is nonsocial because it does not involve other people, and it is reactive because it reacts immediately to the simplest and slightest touches or swipes. In fact, as many parents know, a 2-year-old can pretty easily figure out how to use one without any help or instruction. This is not because 2-year-olds are particularly smart, but because the phone is "smart." It reacts by coming on if the home button is pushed. It reacts by having apps open with only a slight touch on the screen or by having new screens appear with the swipe of a finger. It reacts by talking to you if you talk to it, etc. In fact, such devices build (shape) behavior as evidenced by the fact that children figure out how to use them in pretty short order. Based on what we've learned in this book, because all of your behaviors with a smart phone continue, the smart phone _____*ly* _____*es* these behaviors. Because the reinforcers from the smart phone do not involve people, they are called *automatic*.

Many aspects of the physical environment are reactive: when you push something, it moves; when you pick up something, it comes up, etc. In fact, busy boxes for babies are reactivity devices. Such toys shape and reinforce coordinated behavior such as pushing, pulling, and turning. So, one rule for new parents is: *The more reactive the physical environment is, the quicker and more the baby will learn.* Also, by the way, don't bother buying books or DVDs on how to boost your baby's brain power; creating an enriching, reactive environment will do the trick. Give the infant many things to do that produce tangible effects like sights, sounds, or movement, and you will see their behaviors with those things blossom!

However, the social environment needs to be reactive too, and this is the key to this chapter and this book. In what follows, the examples involve two critical ingredients for you to remember: *1) noticing what behaviors you want and then 2) reinforcing them when they occur.*

Talking and Reading to Your Infant

It is important to know that your baby begins to learn right out of the womb. Actually, even before birth, during the last trimester of pregnancy, the baby's hearing has already developed. The baby begins to learn not only the sound of the mother's voice, but the sounds of the phonemes of the mother's native language. Once the baby is born, it is bathed in the sounds of its native language because it hears a lot of talking many hours each day. And babies born into bilingual or multilingual homes experience a veritable phonemic tower of babble!

Now you might think that because much of the talk the baby hears is not directed at her she does not learn anything from it. But you would be wrong. What she is learning are the sounds of the parents' native language so that when she starts babbling at around 4 to 6 months of age, she will gradually begin to make more and more sounds that resemble those of her parents. Babies born to French-speaking parents begin to babble French sounds, babies born to English-speaking parents begin to babble English sounds, and babies born to Spanish-speaking parents begin to babble Spanish sounds, etc.

Of course, in most typical households, a lot of talk *is* directed to newborns, and research has shown that both the quantity and quality of that talk is crucial for the later development of talking and even intelligence. Researchers have found strong correlations between the sheer number of words infants hear and their own vocabulary development and verbal intelligence. Researchers also have found strong correlations between the number of affirmations, such as when parents reacted positively to the child's behavior (saying "Good job!" "Yes!" etc.), and vocabulary development and verbal intelligence.

Specifically, kids who talked more and had faster vocabulary growth and higher relative IQ scores had parents who 1) talked more; that is, they used more words, more different kinds of words, more multi-clause sentences, more past and future verb tenses, more declaratives, and more questions of all kinds; and 2) responded more to their children's verbal initiations of conversation with affirmative feedback (positive reinforcement).

Children who talked less and had slower vocabulary growth and lower relative IQ scores had parents who 1) talked less, responded less to their children's verbal utterances, and had to initiate verbal interactions relatively more often, and 2) provided more prohibitions ("Don't," "Stop," "Quit," etc.) (punishment) and less affirmative feedback.

So, if you want to maximize your children's verbal intelligence: 1) talk to your child as early and as often as possible, beginning even before he is born; 2) talk a lot with your child about what he is experiencing by using many different words and sentences to describe those experiences; 3) provide positive feedback by repeating, confirming, praising, and approving what your child says; 4) criticize, disapprove, warn, and prohibit infrequently; 5) ask ("Can you . . .?" "Shall we . . .?" "Is it . . .?") rather than tell your child what to do; and 6) reward your child for initiating conversation (with positive reinforcement) so that you have to initiate less.

The take-home point for new parents is: *Talk a lot to your infant, and make sure most of the talk is affirmative.*

Baby Talk

Many parents talk differently to their infants than they do to older children or other adults. This kind of talk, sometimes called motherese, consists of a kind of sing-song way of talking with exaggerated inflection, that is, the pitch and intonation of the parent's voice. Using motherese with your infant attracts her attention and helps her to focus on what you're saying. It is simply an exaggeration of how we talk normally.

Such child-directed speech, however, is different from baby talk. Baby talk (for example, "wawa" instead of water) is probably not recommended because no one ever talks that way as an older child or adult. Not only should you probably not use baby talk with your infant you should probably not reinforce it in your language-learning child. I sometimes see kids who are 6 or 7 years old, and older, who still use baby talk. They do so because that is what their parents reinforced. Such talk in kids may be cute and seem harmless when they are 2 or 3, but when they are old enough to go to school, it can be stigmatizing.

Will Playing Classical Music to Your Infant Make Him or Her Smarter?

Before I leave this section, I want to address the issue of playing music for your unborn baby, newborn, or young infant. Nowadays we hear a lot about the so-called Mozart effect. It may seem intuitive that playing classical music can lead to faster and better brain development and higher intelligence, in particular spatial reasoning performance. The problem is science is not based on intuition. And no studies have been able to replicate the initial report suggesting a relationship. Thus, there is no scientific evidence for the Mozart effect or for any intellectual interventions based on playing classical music for infants. (But try to tell that to the millions who buy those CDs!) Having said that, playing some types of classical music may have a calming effect on your baby and may make it more likely he or she will grow up liking classical music — not a bad thing.

Before going on, try this brief quiz.

Quiz 14

1. True or False? As a parent, you can't start teaching things like potty training, sleeping alone, or even talking until the infant is ready. _____

2. True or False? Newborns have no purposeful or coordinated behavior. _____

3. True or False? Your infant cannot learn right after birth but must wait until they're old enough to understand what you want to teach them. _____

4. The procedure used by the mother to teach her 4-month-old infant to roll over earlier than expected is called _____, because the mother reinforced closer and closer movements to the final one.

5. The kind of environment that includes other people is called the _____ environment, and the kind of environment that does NOT include other people is called the _____ or _____ environment.

6. A _____ environment is one that reacts immediately to behavior.

7. Reinforcers that do not involve people are called _____.

8. The rule is the _____ reactive the physical environment is, the _____ and _____ your baby will learn.

9. True or False? Even though infants begin babbling at around 4 to 6 months of age, they actually begin learning the sounds of their native language at birth, and even before. _____

10. If you want to maximize your children's verbal intelligence, that is, the quality and quantity of their speaking, you should _____ to your child as early and as often as possible; talk a lot about what your child is _____ by using many different words; provide _____ feedback (reinforcement) by repeating, confirming, and praising what they say; and rarely _____ criticize or disapprove of what they say.

Quiz 14 Answers

1. True or False? As a parent, you can't start teaching things like potty training, sleeping alone, or even talking until the infant is ready. *False*

2. True or False? Newborns have no purposeful or coordinated behavior. *True*

3. True or False? Your infant cannot learn right after birth but must wait until they're old enough to understand what you want to teach them. *False*

4. The procedure used by the mother to teach her 4-month-old infant to roll over earlier than expected is called *shaping*, because the mother reinforced closer and closer movements to the final one.

5. The kind of environment that includes other people is called the *social* environment, and the kind of environment that does NOT include other people is called the *nonsocial* or *physical* environment.

6. A *reactive* environment is one that reacts immediately to behavior.

7. Reinforcers that do not involve people are called *automatic*.

8. The rule is the more *reactive* the physical environment is, the *quicker* and *more* your baby will learn.

9. True or False? Even though infants begin babbling at around 4 to 6 months of age, they actually begin learning the sounds of their native language at birth, and even before. *True*

10. If you want to maximize your children's verbal intelligence, that is, the quality and quantity of their speaking, you should *talk*

to your child as early and as often as possible; talk a lot about what your child is *experiencing* by using many different words; provide *immediate* feedback (reinforcement) by repeating, confirming, and praising that they say; and *rarely* criticize or disapprove of what they say.

Part VII – Summing Up

Chapter 15: Summing Up

Chapter 15: Summing Up

To summarize, below is a list of the most important points of the book.

General
1. The kid is always right. There is a cause for the kid's behaviors. (The parent is always right for the same reason.)
2. Kids are not good or bad. Their behavior is.

Reinforcement
3. Reinforcement is an outcome of a behavior that makes that behavior MORE likely to happen again in similar circumstances.
4. Positive reinforcers are *added* after behavior. Negative reinforcers are *subtracted* or taken away after behavior.
5. Automatic reinforcers are not given by another person or not given consciously or intentionally but are the natural byproducts of behavior.
6. Parents and children reinforce each other's behaviors all the time.
7. In order to tell whether some outcome of a behavior is in fact a reinforcer, you must be able to show that it has indeed strengthened (or increased) the behavior it immediately follows under similar circumstances.
8. The more you positively reinforce good, desirable, appropriate behaviors, the less you will have to deal with bad, undesirable, inappropriate behaviors.
9. The best rule to follow to increase your child's self-esteem is to positively reinforce desirable behavior when it occurs *and* tell your child what you liked about their behavior. The self-esteem will follow.
10. The seven factors that contribute to making something work as a reinforcer include: 1) Personalization (the reinforcer must be appropriate for the kid's age); 2)

Motivation (the kid must want the reinforcer); 3) Timing (the reinforcer must immediately follow the behavior); 4) Dependence (the reinforcer must occur ONLY if the behavior occurs); 5) Amount/Effort (the size or amount of the reinforcer must be big enough and the effort of the behavior must be low enough); 6) Schedule (an intermittent schedule generates more persistent behavior); and 7) Consistency (the parents must be consistent in delivering reinforcers for behavior).

11. The more consistently both parents act toward their children, the more consistently the children will act.

12. Grandma's Rule (also known as the Premack Principle) is the opportunity to engage in a more desirable activity ONLY after doing a less desirable activity, which will strengthen the less desirable activity.

Withholding Reinforcement

13. Planned ignoring is NOT giving, or withholding, positive social reinforcement (attention).

14. The more (or longer) the behavior has been positively reinforced with attention, the more it will burst or increase when that attention is withheld, and the longer it will take to decrease.

15. The key to successful planned ignoring is consistency.

Punishment

16. A punisher is any outcome of a behavior that makes the behavior LESS likely to happen under similar circumstances.

17. We punish behavior, not the child.

Steps to Changing Behavior

18. Five Steps to Changing Behavior
    a. Identify the behavior you want to change and the circumstances under which it occurs or under which you would like it to occur.
    b. Select the positive reinforcer you want to use.
    c. Count (or measure) the behavior.
    d. Apply (or withhold) the positive reinforcer.

       e. Evaluate whether the use of positive reinforcement has really increased the targeted behavior.

19. A child does not have to understand what the parents are doing in order for her behavior to change.

Infancy

20. You can begin teaching your child right after they are born.

21. The more reactive the physical and social environments are, the quicker and more the baby will learn.

22. Notice what behaviors you want and then reinforce them when they occur.

23. Talk a lot to your infant, and make sure most of the talk is affirmative.

Appendix I:
Tips and Tidbits

Parents as Models

The following statement, I think, is a truism: "Your children are watching and listening to everything you do and say." This doesn't mean that they are consciously paying attention. It means that they learn by watching and listening to you.

In Chapter 11, I used an example of a boy who pouted and went to his room and slammed his door. I called those behaviors passive aggressive. We might ask how a child would learn to behave in such ways in the first place. It's possible that parents might shape such behaviors over a period of many months or years. Another possibility is that one, or both, of the child's parents behaves in such ways, and the child has learned to behave in similar ways under similar circumstances.

In fact, perhaps the hardest thing to control as a parent is your normal, automatic reactions to various situations. Some of our reactions are healthy and worth modeling, and some are not. You will begin to see yourself in your child's behaviors. Your child will be like a mirror; sometimes you will like what you see, and sometimes you won't. Don't despair; there's probably not much you can do about it, although I certainly encourage you to try.

If you do try, you should begin by identifying the situations in which your reactions are less than satisfactory and then practice either not reacting that way or reacting differently. If you have a spouse or partner, you can enlist him or her to reinforce your behaviors when they are what you would like your child to model; and you can do the same for your spouse or partner.

One of my troublesome reactions is how I react to other drivers when I'm driving. I've been doing that for decades, and I only became acutely aware of it when my toddler started reacting the same way from his car seat in the back. I was aghast. But it's been very hard for me to change those behaviors. And it didn't take too many modeling instances for it to be ingrained in him.

As I mentioned in Chapter 7, if you spank, hit, or scream at your child, he or she may learn to act in similar ways with others. We can see such effects with children who hit or scream at dolls, pets, their friends, and, ultimately, their own children. In essence, they have learned that, under certain circumstances, that is how to deal with others' behavior. They don't think about it and are not aware of it. It has become an automatic way of interacting with others that they learned by watching you.

Answering Your Child

This is a tough one, and one I personally find to be very difficult: answering your child every time he or she says something. We are social beings. We all talk, and many of us talk a lot. We are used to answering other adults when they talk to us. So, when our young children talk to us, we answer them too.

Don't get me wrong, it's a good thing to answer your child when she talks to you because that reinforces more talking. Often kids say things that we really should answer and reinforce. I've given many examples throughout this book. But for the purpose of this section, I want to focus on the seemingly more benign behaviors of debating, negotiating, and arguing. Unless you want your child to grow up to be a trial lawyer or on the debate team, you might want to become aware of when your child argues, debates, or negotiates with you and use planned ignoring for those instances.

This is not easy to do because, as I said, we are used to answering people when they talk to us. For example, when our children ask us why we made a certain decision and we answer, that gives them an opening to further question us. After making this mistake myself for a long time, now when my son asks me why, I don't answer. We think that if we just provide our children with logical answers, they will accept them and stop arguing, debating, or negotiating. That, however, rarely occurs. We often end up, as I have with my son, going back and forth, before I ask myself "What am I doing here?" and stop answering him.

Using a Timer and Counting

Nowadays many people have access to instant timers on their smart phones and other electronic devices. Timers are a great way to get your kids to do what you want because you can make it a game to "beat the clock." If they do what you want and beat the clock, you can deliver praise, such as "Wow, you beat the clock!" Of course, you can also specifically praise them for doing what you asked. Sometimes, just beating the clock, like winning a race, is reinforcement enough. You can also transition to your child setting his or her own timer, which removes you from the equation.

Instead of using a timer, you can just count. When I was a child and my parents would start counting, I knew something bad would happen if I didn't comply before they got to 3. With our son, however, we've been counting to 3 or 5 or 10 since he was old enough to know what counting was, and we never did anything bad if he hadn't at least started what we asked him to do by the time we finished counting. And even by the age of 10, he has rarely, if ever, missed the count. In fact, he uses it as a game—beat the timer—to see if he can comply before we finish counting or before the timer goes off. We never intended it to be that way, but, in retrospect, I would recommend doing that with your child from the beginning.

On the rare occasions when our son did not beat the timer, we had to be more assertive and stand by him until he complied with our request. If our son did what we asked before we finished counting, we would praise and high-five him or just thank him. Some might say we are lucky. After reading this book, I hope you agree it's not luck, but hard work.

Throwing Tantrums

Some parents think that throwing tantrums (crying screaming, throwing things, hitting, etc.) is natural because all kids do it. News flash — they don't! Sometimes, people talk about "the terrible twos" as if all children engage in these behaviors at around 2 years of age. They don't.

Here is the best way to think about throwing tantrums. Ask yourself if a child on a desert island all by herself would ever throw a tantrum. Of course, the answer is no. Now ask yourself why not. The answer is obvious: because it won't get the child anything: no attention from others, no objects like toys or treats. And it won't get them out of having to do anything, such as chores, because there is no one to allow them to escape from or avoid having to do those things.

So, you see, the behaviors involved in throwing tantrums occur because they are reinforced by others (usually parents, but sometimes other relatives and teachers). The tantrum produces certain outcomes (attention, objects, getting out of having to do things) that make the tantrum more likely to occur the next time the child wants any of those things.

The good news is that parents can avoid creating tantrum behaviors or can change (decrease) such behaviors by following the advice laid out in this book and positively reinforcing alternative behaviors when they occur.

How Oppositional and Defiant Behaviors Are Learned

Throughout the book, I've given examples of how some children act out (tantrum, cry, scream, throw things, hit, bite, etc.) when asked to do something, and how their parents let them out of the demand or request. Removing (subtracting) the demand or request is a negative reinforcer for both the kids and the parents. The kids get the demand removed, and the parents get the acting-out behavior removed. Some have called it a reinforcement trap. It's a momentary win-win situation for both parent and child in that they both get what they want. But in the long term, it's a lose-lose situation because both parents and children continue to act badly to get what they want. Researchers have called this coercive control, and children who act in this manner have been called coercive. Even though these kids are called coercive, it's probably more accurate to think of their behavior as coercive. Remember, however, that the kid is always right: the parents built up this behavior by inadvertently reinforcing it.

Many parents think, incorrectly, that their kids will outgrow these behaviors. They won't. In fact, these behaviors will get worse, begin to occur places other than home, and even continue into adulthood.

The point of this section is to alert you to these situations so that you prevent such coercive behaviors from being learned in the first place. The way to do it, as I've suggested previously, is to make sure to use positive reinforcement for compliance and to resist allowing your child's coercive behaviors to let them escape complying with your requests and demands.

ADHD

Millions of kids are diagnosed with ADHD every year, and most are given medication to control the symptoms. But we should ask whether that many kids really do have a disorder, which suggests some kind of abnormal brain function. As a way of being skeptical, think about how most typical young children behave. They are active, easily distractable, and impulsive. Then, when they are about 5 or 6 years of age, we put them in an environment where they are expected to sit still and concentrate for long periods of time. It is called school. Moreover, classrooms are often boring, especially when compared to the pace of video games, television, etc., that kids have already spent years with. Also, the work is either too easy or too difficult, depending on the child. The circumstances are ripe for the behaviors they already have a tendency to engage in to occur.

In the classroom, such behaviors are disruptive. Often, teachers only, or mostly, pay attention to children when they are behaving in such ways, by saying things like "Sit down, Daniel!" or "Pay attention, Cora!" Or the kids get out of having to do schoolwork. As mentioned in the previous section, these kids are exerting coercive control over the teachers. Teachers are usually not trained to deal with such behaviors in a manner consistent with the approach in this book. When teachers are at their wits' end, they refer these children to the school nurse or tell the parents to have their child evaluated for ADHD. Often, these kids are diagnosed with ADHD and put on medication.

There is a significant amount of research showing that there is much less ADHD in classrooms that are engaging, fast paced, and designed so that students can move at their own pace. Unfortunately, not many classrooms are structured in such a way.

So, teachers are left having to teach and to manage behavior. The point is that not only are these behaviors not inevitable, they are treatable with the methods described in this book.

Appendix II:
5 Myths Regarding Positive Reinforcement

Over the years, several objections to using positive reinforcement have been voiced. Many of them are based on misunderstandings of what positive reinforcement is. Most of them do not have merit, but they garner a lot of attention, largely from authors who do not understand the experimental basis of positive reinforcement, or from unknowledgeable media who disseminate misinformation because it sells newspapers, magazines, or ads on social media sites. As a result, several myths about positive reinforcement live on in some circles. I will try to briefly list and dispel a few of the more popular myths.

Myth 1: *Reinforcement Doesn't Work with Humans*
This is simply wrong, as hundreds of experiments and thousands of applied studies have shown. On the contrary, reinforcement is responsible for more human behavior than that of any other species. That is why I call humans the *learning animal*. Reinforcement is ubiquitous with human behavior because of how certain parts of our brains have evolved (See Appendix III).

Myth 2: *Using Positive Reinforcement Is Bribery*
According to Webster's Ninth New Collegiate Dictionary, a bribe is defined as "money or favor given or promised to a person in a position of trust to influence his judgment or conduct." By definition, the bribe is given *before* the behavior, and, by implication, the behavior is usually of questionable morality. A reinforcer, on the other hand is given _____ the behavior, and while the behavior can be either good or bad, we hope to use positive reinforcement to increase good behavior. Using positive

reinforcement is no more bribery than praising someone for a good job, saying "Thank you," or paying someone for a day's work.

Myth 3: *Using Positive Reinforcement Is Unnatural*
  Some people complain that using positive reinforcement intentionally, as this book suggests, is contrived and unnatural. Part of this charge is true — that it is contrived — but it is not a bad thing. The alternative to using positive reinforcement intentionally to increase desirable behavior is not to be aware of how we use it unintentionally to teach or increase undesirable or self-destructive behavior. After all, we use other scientific principles and knowledge intentionally to change things — such as using chemistry and biology to create new medicines that improve people's health. Why not use a science of behavior to improve people's behavior, self-esteem, and happiness?

Myth 4: *Using Positive Reinforcement Is Manipulative*
  This objection is similar to the charge that using positive reinforcement is unnatural, but it goes one step further to claim that it is manipulative. This charge is true and not true. According to Webster's Ninth New Collegiate Dictionary, there are two definitions of *to manipulate*. One is "to control or play upon by artful, unfair, or insidious means, especially to one's own advantage," and the other is "to manage or utilize skillfully." The charge that using positive reinforcement is manipulative is true if it means that positive reinforcement is used to manage skillfully. According to this meaning, and the intention of this book, you can learn to use positive reinforcement to manage behavior in a skillful manner. But if the charge refers to the first definition, then it is not true. Using positive reinforcement intentionally is not insidious or unfair; it is used to the advantage of both the user and the recipient.

Myth 5: *Using Positive Reinforcement Undermines Intrinsic Motivation*
  The objection to using positive reinforcement that has received the most press is that it undermines intrinsic motivation and, thus, actually decreases behavior. Entire books and scholarly

papers have been written about the falsity of this topic. But for the present purposes, I will answer and dismiss the charge by quoting from an article by Robert Eisenberger and Judy Cameron published in the *American Psychologist* in 1996: "The myth that offering a reward reduces creativity and the intrinsic interest of a task has grown far beyond what the data can support. Rewards can increase creativity, and negative effects of rewards occur under highly restricted and easily avoided conditions." Notice, however, that they use the term reward, not reinforcement. Reinforcement is defined by the fact that it increases behavior under similar circumstances. In fact, contrary to the criticism, reinforcement can actually increase what is termed intrinsic motivation. When used skillfully, the behaviors taught initially with reinforcement do become intrinsically rewarding; that is, such behaviors produce their own automatic reinforcement.

Appendix III:
Reinforcement and the Brain

Many people nowadays like to throw around terms having to do with the brain. Phrases like "executive function" have become popularized. Most of those who throw around these terms are not neuroscientists and know very little, if anything, about the brain. But it makes them sound scientific and knowledgeable if they use terms like executive function or amygdala. There is no question that the composition of our brain makes it possible for reinforcement to work the way it does. Also, the large size of the cortex of our brain (compared to other animals) is related to the fact that it is very flexible — some use the word "plastic" — meaning it can be changed. The primary source of changes in the cortex is certain experiences psychologists call *learning*. Although the biggest percentage change in the connections of the cortex due to learning happens during the first 3 years of life, we all know that learning can occur until we are very old. Most of our learning and, thus, changes in the cortex occur through the use of reinforcement.

Research using PET scans has shown that the most active parts of the newborn's brain are those involved in sensing (hearing, seeing, etc.) and movement. The areas responsible for coordinated behavior, from reaching and grasping to walking, show very little activity. And the parts of the brain associated with memories show almost no activity because, well, there are not yet any memories (learning hasn't taken place yet). The same research shows dramatic development of areas of the brain associated with learning and memory as the infant begins to interact with her environment, in other words, once learning through reinforcement begins to occur.

The same research also shows that there is what is called a sensitive period in early childhood during which stimulation from a reactive environment will produce the most learning, as discussed in Chapter 14.

Knowing about the brain is unnecessary to building good behavior and self-esteem in your child. In fact, if you follow the advice offered in this book, you will be building neural connections in your child's brain as well as good behavior and self-esteem.

Suggested Readings

Below is a short list of readings that parents and practitioners may find useful.

Azrin, N., & Foxx, R. M. (1974; 2019). *Toilet Training in Less Than a Day*. New York, NY: Gallery Books.
An extremely popular book that has sold millions of copies shows how to toilet train your toddler in less than a day using some of the methods discussed in this book.

Chugani, H. T. (2004). Fine-tuning the baby brain. *Cerebrum, 6,* 33-48.
A somewhat difficult article that shows that the infant's brain is extremely plastic and that learning experiences, such as those presented in this book, have their biggest impact during this sensitive period of early childhood.

Clark. L. F. (2017). *SOS Help for Parents: A Practical Guide for Handling Common Everyday Behavior Problems*. Bowling Green, KY: Parents Press.
This is the best book for those interested in how to use time-out most effectively. It also discusses how to positively reinforce desirable behavior and ignore undesirable behavior.

Eisenberger, R., & Cameron, J. (1996). Detrimental effects of reward: Reality or myth? *American Psychologist, 51*(11), 1153–1166.
This article is just one of many that provides a correct perspective on the somewhat straw-man issue of intrinsic vs. extrinsic rewards.

Engleman, S., Haddoz, P., & Bruner, P. (1983). *How to Teach Your Child to Read in 100 Easy Lessons*. New York: Touchstone.
This book does what it promises: teach your child to read at about the second-grade level in two months. We used it with our son, and it delivers. All beginning reading teachers should use this book instead of whatever they are doing.

Friman P. C., Hoff, K. E., Schnoes, C., Freeman, K. A., Woods, D. W., Blum N. (1999). The bedtime pass: An approach to bedtime crying and leaving the room. *Archives of Pediatric and Adolescent Medicine, 153*: 1027 1029.
One of two studies that describe the bedtime pass.

Hart, B., & Risley, T. R. (2003). The early catastrophe: The 30 million word gap by age 3. *The American Educator, 27*(1), 4-9.
This article describes the seminal longitudinal research project carried out by the authors that documented in 40 American families across three different socioeconomic groups the relation between parent talk and child talk and, later, child verbal fluency.

Hupp, S., Stary, A., & Jewell, J. (2017). Science vs. silliness for parents: Debunking the myths of child psychology. *Skeptical Inquirer, 41(1)*, 44-47.
This article does a nice job of debunking many of the myths of child psychology.

Miltenberger, R.G. (2016). *Behavior Modification: Principles and Procedures* (6th Ed.), Chapter 12. Boston, MA: Cengage.
Chapter 12 of this textbook presents a good description of Behavioral Skills Training by the researcher who is one of the pioneers of the method.

Miltenberger, R. G., Sanchez, S., Valbuena, D. (2020). Pediatric Prevention: Teaching Safety Skills. *Pediatr Clin North Am. 67(3)*, 573-584. doi: 10.1016/j.pcl.2020.02.011. PMID: 32443995.
This article describes the use of BST to teach safety skills to children.

Moore, B. A., Friman, P. C. Fruzzetti, A. E., MacAleese, K. (April 2007). Brief report: Evaluating the bedtime pass program for child resistance to bedtime—A randomized, controlled trial, *Journal of Pediatric Psychology*, 32(3), 283-287.
The other study on the effectiveness of the bedtime pass.

Pan-Skadden, J., Wilder, D.A., Sparling, J., Severtson, E., Donaldson, J., Postma, N., Beavers, G, & Neidert, P.

(2009). The use of behavioral skills training and in-situ training to teach children to solicit help when lost: A preliminary investigation. *Education and Treatment of Children 32(3)*, 359-370.

This article nicely illustrates how BST was used to teach children to solicit help when lost, a very important skill.

Prior, K. (1984). *Don't Shoot the Dog: The New Art of Teaching and Training*. New York: Bantam.

As the title suggests, this book talks about how to use the methods of positive reinforcement to teach and train without coercion.

Reid, J. B., Patterson, G. R., & Snyder, J. (Eds.). (2002). *Antisocial Behavior in Children and Adolescents: A Developmental Analysis and Model for Intervention*. American Psychological Association.

This book describes proven approaches to "reducing the occurrence and severity of antisocial behavior" based on Patterson's model of the coercive family process and the negative reinforcement trap.

Ruff, M. E. (2005). Attention deficit disorder and stimulus use: An epidemic of modernity. *Clinical Pediatrics, 44*, 557-563.

This article nicely shows how ADHD may not be all that it is cracked up to be.

Schlinger, H. D. (1995). *A Behavior-Analytic View of Child Development*. New York: Plenum.

This is my book on infant and child development from a behavior-analytic perspective. It was written for students of behavior analysis, so it is not for beginners.

Schlinger, H. (August 2007) ADHD. *Education.com*. http://www.education.com/magazine/article/Why_ADHD_Often_Pops_Second_Grade/

Schlinger, H. (August 2007) Writing: It takes practice. *Education.com*.http://www.education.com/magazine/article/Writing_Success_Behavior/

These two very brief articles illustrate with two examples what I've tried to convey in this book.

Schlinger, H. D. (2020). The impact of B. F. Skinner's science of operant learning on early childhood research, theory, treatment, and care. *Early Childhood Development and Care.*

In this article, I try to show the extensive impact of the science that the behavioral psychologist B. F. Skinner discovered on child development research, theory, treatment, and care.

Sutherland, A. (2008). *What Shamu Taught Me About Life, Love, and Marriage.* New York, NY: Random House.

This book is an elaboration of Sutherland's *New York Times* article, "*What Shamu taught me about a happy marriage,*" (https://www.nytimes.com/2019/10/11/style/modern-love-what-shamu-taught-me-happy-marriage.html), which was one of the most emailed *Times* articles ever. In it, Sutherland shows how she used the principles discussed in the present book to change the behavior of her husband.

About the Author

Henry D. (Hank) Schlinger Jr. was born and raised in Dallas, Texas. He received his B.S. and M.A. in experimental psychology from Southern Methodist University and his Ph.D. in psychology with a concentration in Applied Behavior Analysis (ABA) from Western Michigan University. After receiving his Ph.D., Dr. Schlinger completed a two-year post-doctoral fellowship in behavioral pharmacology, also at Western Michigan University. Before moving to Los Angeles in 1999, Dr. Schlinger was a tenured full professor in the Psychology Department at Western New England University in Springfield, Massachusetts. He has been Professor of Psychology at California State University, Los Angeles (CSULA) since 2006 and directed the Master of Science Program in ABA from 2007-2014.

Dr. Schlinger has authored (or co-authored) three books: *Psychology: A behavioral overview* (1990), *A behavior-analytic view of child development* (1995) (which was translated into Japanese), and *Introduction to scientific psychology* (1998). He has published more than 80 scholarly articles, book reviews, and commentaries, including several on child development, in more than 35, mostly peer-reviewed, journals. In addition, he wrote a Behavioral Health column in *Arroyo Monthly* magazine for more than two years, addressing numerous behavioral problems, many in children. He has also written columns for Education.com and is often quoted by other writers.

Dr. Schlinger is invited to speak all over the world. He has presented at a number of agencies all over the country that serve families of children with autism and related disorders. He also regularly presents webinars on a variety of topics related to behavior analysis, including child development.

Dr. Schlinger serves on several journal editorial boards, is a Trustee of the Cambridge Center for Behavioral Studies and serves on the advisory boards of the B. F. Skinner Foundation and The Venus Project.

He is also an accomplished songwriter, guitarist, and singer, whose CD, *One More Invention* is available on Spotify, Apple Music, and Amazon.com, among other music sites.

Dr. Schlinger lives in the quiet, serene hills of Glendale, California, north of Los Angeles, with his wife, Julie Riggott, an editor and writer, and their 10-year-old son, Haydn, who is a talented, affectionate, and mostly well-behaved and happy kid.

Made in the USA
Columbia, SC
19 December 2024

49963904R00115